Blueprint:
Understanding Your Responsibilities to Meet DOD NIST 800-171

The Definitive Cybersecurity Contract Guide

INCLUDES the most comprehensive NIST-based "Compliance Checklist"

Mark A. Russo
CISSP-ISSAP, CISO

DEDICATION

This book is dedicated to the cybersecurity men and women that protect and defend the Information Systems of this great Nation.

This is also dedicated to my family who have been supportive of my endeavors to plunge into writing as not just a hobby but a calling to make the world a better and safer place.

Copyright 2018, by Syber Risk LLC

LEGAL STUFF

Blueprint: Understanding Your Responsibilities to Meet DOD NIST 800-171

Table of Contents

INTRODUCTION

DOD Cybersecurity gets serious

This book is created to help the small to big business owner in meeting the newest in cybersecurity contracting requirements to conduct business with the Department of the Defense (DOD). It is intended to assist companies and their Information Technology (IT) staffs' on how to best address the DOD challenges of meeting the demands of the 2016 National Institute of Standards and Technology (NIST) Special Publication (SP) 800-171, revision 1, *Protecting Controlled Unclassified Information in Nonfederal Information Systems and Organizations*. This includes compliance with the Federal Acquisition Regulation (FAR) clause 52.204-21 and its companion DOD supplement, the Defense Federal Acquisition Regulation Supplement (DFARS), and its specific clause, 252.204-7012.

To participate in any current or future DOD contract effort, either as a prime or subcontractor, a company is now REQUIRED to be fully NIST 800-171 revision 1 compliant. As of December 31, 2017, any company wishing to do business with DOD is required to meet the **110** NIST-based security controls. Companies can implement these security solutions either directly or by using outside, third-party, "managed services" to satisfy the protection requirements of Controlled Unclassified Information (CUI)/Covered Defense Information (CDI). NIST publications while not previously mandatory for "nonfederal entities," NIST 800-171 rev. 1, is the first time that a federal agency has mandated nonfederal agencies, vis a vis, private companies, comply with this federal-specific publication.

"Nonfederal" organizations, such as businesses, and their internal IT systems processing, storing, or transmitting CUI may be required to comply with this publication. In the case of DOD, that suggestion is *now* mandatory.

CUI is not considered national security level information such as **Confidential**, **Secret**, or **Top Secret**. The former DOD terminology for CUI or CDI was predominantly categorized as **For Official Use Only** (FOUO). This data is considered sensitive, but not requiring more stringent security or control mechanisms as with national security information. Basic CUI/CDI may include employee records, Personal Health Information (PHI), or Personally Identifiable Information (PII) protected by federal and state laws. CDI is more specific to the operational and support functions required by DOD to perform its national mission.

Why pursue an expansion of NIST-based cybersecurity standards?

Ongoing intrusions into critical federal systems point to the ever agile and highly impactful effects of cyber-threats worldwide. Reports of the large volumes of personal data exfiltrated from the Office of Personnel Management (OPM), and intrusions into seemingly highly protected networks of the DOD, highlights the need for change. "For nearly a week, some 4,000-key military and civilian personnel working for the Joint Chiefs of Staff [had] lost access to their unclassified email after what is now believed to be an intrusion into the critical Pentagon server that handles that email network..." (Starr, B. 2015, July 31. *Military still dealing with cyberattack 'mess'.* Retrieved from CNN.com: http://www.cnn.com/2015/07/31/politics/defense-department-computer-intrusion-email-server/)

The need to implement and enhance the Risk Management Framework (RMF) based upon NIST's cybersecurity focused 800-series continues to be highly debated. The challenge has been about whether to expand the NIST RMF "framework" beyond the federal government's multiple IT security boundaries. What if the federal government mandated its applicability to the private sector? Can the expansion of the NIST 800-series, to include specifically NIST 800-171, provide a better means to protect the Nation's sensitive data?

This also includes enhancing laws and regulations to increase corporate and business cybersecurity protections; this comprises current laws such as the Federal Information Security Management Act (FISMA) of 2002 and updated by Congress in 2014. These laws, regulations and processes will hopefully improve and protect the critical infrastructures and sensitive data stored within the physical boundaries of the US and its vital corporations. Presumably such an evolution will better protect the US's vital and sensitive data from both internal and foreign state actors desiring to harm the US.

FISMA was written by Congress to reduce the effectiveness of cyber-attacks against the federal government and its vast IT infrastructure. FISMA and other cybersecurity laws provide a needed method to enhance oversight of information security applications, systems, and networks. FISMA further explicitly sought to "...provide a comprehensive framework for ensuring the effectiveness of information security controls over information resources that support Federal operations and assets" (US Government. (2002). *Federal Information Security Management Act of 2002 (44 U.S.C. §§ 3541-3549).* Retrieved from NIST: http://csrc.nist.gov/drivers/documents/FISMA-final.pdf)).

In 2014, DOD internally adopted the NIST RMF 800-series as the standard. The overall effort has become the current DOD direction and guidance to more effectively protect its own critical IT infrastructure, and to expand beyond its boundaries to protect *its* data transmitted into the private sector.

NIST 800-171 rev. 1 is that first attempt for DOD that applies to vendors and contractors to ensure CUI/CDI is properly protected from threats. It is further mandated that information about a company's business specific to the DOD is protected from compromise or exploit; that is modification, loss or destruction. DOD is attempting to ensure a basic effort is executed to protect the company's own internal CUI as well as co-mingled DOD information that is created as part of the company's normal business operations.

What does compliance mean for DOD?

This book describes both the methods and means to "self-assess" and provide requisite proof to, for example, the Contracting Officer or designated representative that a company meets these requirements. There are **110** explicit security controls from NIST 800-171 extracted from NIST's core cybersecurity document, NIST 800-53, *Security and Privacy Controls for Federal Information Systems and Organizations*, that are considered vital; this is a highly pared down set of controls to meet that requirement based on over a thousand potential controls offered from NIST 800-53 revision 4. This more expansive set of controls is used by DOD to protect all DOD systems from its jet fighters to its vast personnel databases.

This book is intended to focus business owners and their IT support staff on the minimum and more complete suggested answers to each of these controls.   Companies fortunately only need to focus on how to best address these "minimal" controls to the government—and, it more thoughtfully will help the business protect its own sensitive data and Intellectual Property (IP).

The **People, Process and Technology (PPT) Model** is the recommended guidance for answering many of the controls within NIST 800-171. While all solutions will not necessarily require a **technological** answer, consideration of the **people** (e.g., who? what skill sets? etc.) and **process** (e.g., notifications to senior management, action workflows, etc.) will meet many of the response requirements. Refer to Control 3.6.1 that provides example questions that could be offered and answered when using the People-Process-Technology (PPT) model. The best responses will typically include the types and kinds of people assigned to oversee the control, the process or procedures that identify the workflow that will ensure that the control is met, and in many cases, the technology that will answer the control in part or in full.

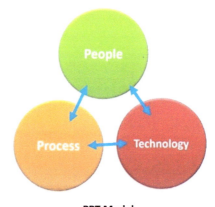

PPT Model

What's the minimum proof of a company's cybersecurity posture?

The basis of NIST 800-171 is that contractors provide adequate security on all covered contractor Information Systems (IS). Typically, the minimum requirement to demonstrate control implementation is through **documentation**. Another term that is used throughout this book is an **artifact**. An artifact is any representation to an independent third-party assessor that clearly shows compliance with a specific security control. It is a major part of the proof that a business owner would provide DOD.

The common term for the collection of all applicable and supporting artifacts is the Body of Evidence (BOE). The major items required for the BOE includes three major items:

1. **Company Policy** or **Procedure.** *For the purposes of this book these terms are used interchangeably.* Essentially any direction provided to internal employees and subcontractors that are enforceable under United States (US) labor laws and Human Resource (HR) direction. It is recommended that such a policy or procedure artifact be a *singular* collection of how the company addresses each of the 110 security controls.

REMINDER: All policy or procedure requirements are best captured in a single business policy or procedure guide. This should address the controls aligned with the security control families

---

2. **System Security Plan (SSP).** This is a standard cybersecurity document. It describes the company's overall IT infrastructure to include hardware and software lists. Where appropriate, suggestions of additional artifacts that should be included in this document and duplicated into a DOD standard SSP format will be recommended. (See *System Security Plan (SSP) Template and Workbook: A Supplement to Understanding Your Responsibility to Meet NIST 800-171* on Amazon®)

3. **Plans of Action and Milestones (POAM).** This describes any control that the company cannot fix or fully demonstrate its full compliance with the control. It provides an opportunity for a company to delay addressing a difficult to implement technical solution or because cost may be prohibitive.

   POAMs should always have an expected completion date and defined interim milestones (typically monthly) that describes the actions leading to a full resolution or implementation of the control. *POAMs typically should not be for more than a year, however, a critical hint, a company can request an* <u>extension</u> *multiple times if unable to fully meet the control.*

When working with the government simple and consistent always helps through a very young and undefined process

---

More About Artifacts and POAMs?

Other artifacts that will are suggested including **screen captures.** All current Operating Systems (OS) include a "print screen" function where the text or image is captured, placed in temporary computer memory and can be easily inserted into other locations or hard copy printed; IT personnel should use this function to show, for example, policy settings and system logging (audit) data. When in doubt, always have some form of graphical representation to show the government.

The POAM will be used where the business cannot meet or address the control either for technical reasons, "we don't have a Data at Rest (DAR) encryption program," or cost, "we plan to purchase the DAR solution No Later Than April 1, 2019." POAMs should include **milestones**; milestones should describe what will be accomplished overtime to prepare for the full implementation of the control in the future. What will the business do in the interim to address the control? This could include, for example, other **mitigation** responses of using improved physical security controls, such as a 24-7 guard force, the addition of a steel-door to prevent entry to the main computer servers or improved and enforceable policies that have explicit repercussions upon personnel.

POAMs will always have a defined end date. Typically, it is either within 90 days, 6 months, or a year in length. For DOD, one year should be the maximum date; however, the business, as part of this fledgling process can request an extension to the POAM past the "planned" end date. RMF affords such flexibilities; don't be afraid to exercise them as appropriate. (See Access Control (AC) for a sample template).

Finally, there are number of standard NIST formats and templates designed to make this effort easier. Suggest using a Security Control Traceability Matrix (SCTM) for traceability of the controls and to furthermore create a "test plan" that demonstrates and answers questions about a business' self-assessment effort; this is typically in the form of a spreadsheet that can be better filtered and manipulated for ongoing assessment purposes and updates.

__Special Note about this Gray Version:__ This version is printed without color to provide a lower cost and more accessible to a greater audience. In 2018 the Federal Acquisition Regulation (FAR) Committee IS EXPECTED to require a greater implementation of NIST 800-171 throughout the Federal Government.   This book can also be used by companies required to comply with cybersecurity changes impacting all federal executive agencies of the US Government.

ALL THINGS CONSIDERED

How to use this book?

This book is specifically aligned with the requirements outlined in NIST 800-171's security control families and their specific controls that NIST (and DOD) have deemed vital to secure CUI/CDI. It will help the business to follow the requirements, and additionally will assist them to deliver a cogent response to the government.

Getting into a cybersecurity mind-set

The focus is to provide the mental approach and technical understanding of what the control is (and what it is not). The first paragraph describes a MINIMUM ANSWER. This is what is needed to prepare a base answer for a minimal and acceptable level of response. Mainly, the solutions here require policy or procedural documents that describe to the government how the business will ensure this control will be met; if just trying to get through the process expeditiously, this paragraph will be enough to secure an approval.

If there is a greater desire to further understand the process, and demonstrate a more substantial solution, the paragraph, MORE COMPLETE ANSWER is designed to provide more depth. It is intended to more completely describe to the business owner how to better show an understanding to DOD its implementation of NIST 800-171.

Also, for clarification, the *Basic Security Requirement* **heading** is what is typically described as the **Common Control** for that control family. It is best just to understand it is the major control for the respective control family (see the **NIST 800-171 SECURITY REQUIREMENT FAMILIES**). The *Derived Security Requirements* can be considered more as supplemental and "more granular" requirements for the "parent" control. Depending on the types and kinds of data stored, these controls in the more *classic* NIST 800-53 publication can include hundreds of other controls; DOD has fortunately deemed only 110 controls as necessary.

FAMILY	FAMILY
(AC) Access Control	(MP) Media Protection
(AT) Awareness and Training	(PS) Personnel Security
(AU) Audit and Accountability	(PP) Physical Protection
(CM) Configuration Management	(RA) Risk Assessment
(IA) Identification and Authentication	(SA) Security Assessment
(IR) Incident Response	(SC) System and Communications Protection
(MA) Maintenance	(SI) System and Information Integrity

NIST 800-171 SECURITY REQUIREMENT FAMILIES

Tailoring-out Controls Possibilities

The 2016 version update to NIST 800-171, revision 1, provides an *inadequate* direction on the matter of **control tailoring**. It states in Appendix E that there are three primary criteria for the removal of a security control (or control enhancement):

> • **The control is uniquely federal (i.e., primarily the responsibility of the federal government):** DOD directly provides the control to the company. While possible, expect this to not typically occur.

> • **The control is not directly related to protecting the confidentiality of CUI/CDI:** This will also not apply since all these controls were originally chosen to protect the confidentiality of all CUI/CDI. That's why this book exists to better explain how to address these controls which are for the most part all required.

> • **The control is expected to be routinely satisfied by Nonfederal Organizations (NFO) without specification:** In other words, the control is expected to be met by the NFO, i.e., the company. That is, you and your IT team.

Tailoring is completely allowed and recommended where appropriate. Within the NIST cybersecurity framework the concept of **tailoring-out** of a control is desirable where technically or operationally it cannot be reasonably applied. This will require technical certainty that the control is Non-Applicable (N/A). Under this opportunity, if the company's IT architecture does not contain within its **security boundary** the technology where such a control would be required to be applied then the control is identified as N/A.

For example, where the business has no Wi-Fi network in its security boundary, it can advise the government that any controls addressing the security of its Wi-Fi would be a N/A control. The business cannot nor have reason to implement this control because it currently doesn't allow Wi-Fi networks or any presence of such equipment such as Wi-Fi routers, antennas, etc. The control would be marked as **compliant** and annotated as N/A at the time of the self-assessment. It would still be required to identify that Wi-fi is not currently authorized in the company's cybersecurity procedure guide or policy.

Tailoring-out can be your friend

ACCESS CONTROL (AC)
The most technical, complex and vital

Access Control (AC) is probably the most technical and most vital security control family within the cybersecurity process. It is designed to focus computer support personnel, System Administrators (SA), or similar IT staff, on the technical security protections of critical data. This will include any CUI/CDI and internal sensitive data maintained by the company's IT infrastructure and maintained by the company as part of doing business with DOD. If making investments in cybersecurity infrastructure upgrades, the *AC control will provide the greatest Return on Investment.*

Also, it is important to confirm whether either a technical solution is not already embedded in the current IT system. Many times, controls are ignored, captured by policy, or a POAM is developed, even though some base capabilities to address the control are already resident in the base system or more particularly within the network Operating System (OS). Also check for accessory applications provided by the OS manufacturer to determine whether a no-cost solution is already resident. Ask the IT staff to confirm whether there is an existing technical solution as part of the system to avoid spending additional dollars for capabilities already in place.

Where cost is currently prohibitive to implement, a POAM is an acceptable but temporary solution. (See *Introduction* for a more thorough description on preparing proper DOD POAMs). If unable to address the control during the company's "self-assessment" effort, then be prepared to formulate a Plans of Action and Milestone (POAM). (***Writing an Effective POAM*** will be a subsequent supplement to this book to be released on Amazon®; we will be using the "Intelligence Cycle" as a model to manage the lifecycle of an active POAM as part of that release).

© S.R. White - Intelligence Cycle Approach to the POAM Lifecycle

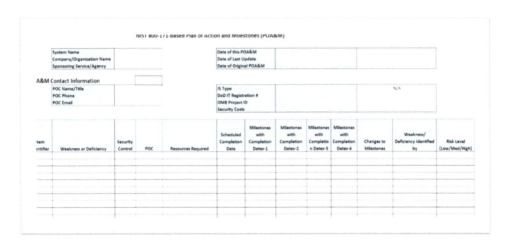

Sample POAM Template

Basic Security Requirements:

3.1.1 Limit information system access to authorized users, processes acting on behalf of authorized users, or devices (including other information systems).

MINIMUM ANSWER: Address this control in the business policy/procedural document. (See example procedure below).

It should identify the types of users and what level of access they are authorized. Typically, there are **general users** who have regular daily access to the corporate system data, and **elevated/privileged users**.

Elevated/privileged users are usually limited to, for example, System Administrators (SA), Database Administrators (DBA), and other designated Help Desk IT support staff personnel who manage the back-office care of the system; these users usually have **root access**. Root access provides what is more typically described as **super-user** access. These individuals should be highly and regularly screened. These individuals need to be regularly assessed or audited by senior corporate designated personnel.

MORE COMPLETE ANSWER: This should include screen captures that show a sample of employees and their types and kinds of access rights. This could include their read, write, edit, delete, etc., **rights** typically controlled by an assigned SA.

We have provided an example of a suggested procedure for this control:

> EXAMPLE PROCEDURE: *The company has defined two types of authorized users. There are **general users**, those that require normal daily access to company automated resources, and **privileged users**, employees with elevated privileges required to conduct regular back-office care and maintenance of corporate assets and Information Technology (IT) systems. Access to the company's [example] financial, ordering and human resource systems will be restricted to those general users with a need, based upon their duties, to access these systems. Immediate supervisors will validate their need and advise the IT Help Desk to issue appropriate access credentials [logon identification and password] after completing "Cybersecurity Awareness Training." User credentials will not be shared and...."*

3.1.2 Limit information system access to the types of transactions and functions that authorized users are permitted to execute.

MINIMUM ANSWER: Address this control in the business policy/procedural document. It should identify the types of transactions and what level is allowed for authorized users. Elevated or privileged users have access to back-office maintenance and care of the network such as account creation, database maintenance, etc.; privileged users can also have general access, but their privileges should be segregated by different logins and passwords for audit purposes.

MORE COMPLETE ANSWER: This could include a screen capture that shows a sample of employees and their types and kinds of rights. This would include their read, write, edit, delete, etc., rights typically controlled by assigned SA. The SA should be able to provide the hardcopy print outs for inclusion into the final submission packet to the DOD contract office or their designated recipient.

Derived (Supplemental) Security Requirements:

3.1.3 Control the flow of CUI in accordance with approved authorizations.

MINIMUM ANSWER: Companies typically use **flow control** policies and technologies to manage the movement of CUI/CDI throughout the IT architecture; flow control is based on the types of information.

In terms of procedural updates, discussion for the corporate documents should address several areas of concern: 1) That only authorized personnel within the company with the requisite need-to-know are provided access; 2) appropriate security measures are in place to include encryption while Data is in Transit (DIT); 3) what are the procedures for handling internal employees who violate these company rules?; and, 4) how does the company alert DOD if there is external access (hackers) to its IT infrastructure and its CUI/CDI?

MORE COMPLETE ANSWER: Addressing this control can further be demonstrated by implementing training (See Awareness and Training (AT) control) as a form of **mitigation**; mitigation are other supporting efforts, not just technical, that can reduce the effects if a threat exploits this control. The company could also include risk from insider threats (See Control 3.2.3 for discussion of "insider threat.") by requiring employees to complete Non-disclosure (NDA) and non-compete agreements (NCA). These added measures *reduce or mitigate the risk to the IT infrastructure*. They should also address employees that depart, resign, or are terminated by the company; the consideration is for disgruntled employees that may depart the company with potentially sensitive CUI/CDI.

Flow control could also be better shown to a DOD assessor in terms of a technical solution. This could be further demonstrated by using encryption for DIT and Data at Rest (DAR). These encryption requirements within NIST 800-171 necessitate differing technical solutions, and Federal Information Processing Standards (FIPS) 140-2 compliance; see Control 3.13.11 for more detail.

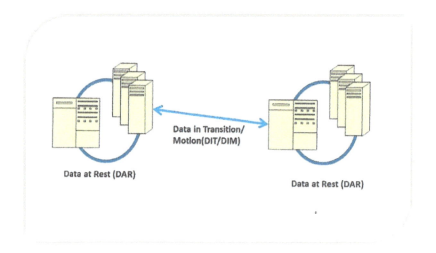

Data in Transition/
Motion(DIT/DIM)

Data at Rest (DAR)

Data at Rest (DAR)

Data at Rest (DAR) versus Data in Transit/Motion (DIT/DIM) Conceptual Diagram

The answer could also include weekly reviews of access logs. Typically, IT support personnel or the SA would conduct recurring audits. If anomalies are detected, what is the procedure to alert senior management to personnel attempting access to CUI/CDI and other sensitive data? This offers a greater demonstration of company security measures to DOD representatives.

3.1.4 Separate the duties of individuals to reduce the risk of malevolent activity without collusion.

MINIMUM ANSWER: This should be described in the corporate cybersecurity procedural document and should identify roles and responsibilities of how oversight will be executed. When this is difficult, based upon the size and limited IT personnel, a POAM is highly recommended.

The POAM should suggest other ways used to mitigate such a **risk**, and potentially look at both human and automated means to better address in the future.

MORE COMPLETE ANSWER: Individuals should be assigned *in-writing* and their roles and responsibilities. This could also include the reporting thresholds of unauthorized activities and who is alerted internal threats; this would better provide a more defined solution. It also could address Human Resource (HR) challenges when such incidents occur and provide a means of action against violators of corporate policy.

3.1.5 Employ the principle of least privilege, including for specific security functions and privileged accounts.

MINIMUM ANSWER: The principle of least privilege is an important cybersecurity tenet. The concept of least privilege is about allowing only authorized access for users and processes that they have direct responsibility. It is limited to only a necessary level of access to accomplish tasks for specific business functions. This should be described in the corporate cybersecurity policy document. This should also be part of basic user agreements to include what is described in DOD terminology an **Acceptable Use Policy** (AUP).

MORE COMPLETE ANSWER: Much like the controls described above, a sampling of employees' print-outs or screen captures could show selected and authorized individual rights. A sampling, especially of privileged users, and their assigned roles within the company's IT infrastructure would be a target of potential third-party DOD assessors. This would be used by assessors to support the developing NIST 800-171 certification process.

3.1.6 Use non-privileged accounts or roles when accessing nonsecurity functions.

MINIMUM ANSWER: It is best to always first answer controls from a policy or procedural solution. Essentially, this is preventing "general users" from accessing the corporate infrastructure and creating accounts, deleting databases, or elevating their privileges to gain access to both CUI/CDI and sensitive corporate data. This is about providing the least amount of access and privilege based upon the duties assigned. Companies will see the control below that mandates a separation not just of duties, but access as well based upon position and a clear need-to-know.

MORE COMPLETE ANSWER: The more complete answer could be through automated solutions that monitor access of other than security functions such as password resets, account creation, etc. This could include logging and review of all system access. It could also include automated tools that restrict access based upon a user's rights. These technical settings within the tool are established by company policy and monitored by, for example, the local SA.

3.1.7 Prevent non-privileged users from executing privileged functions and audit the execution of such functions.

MINIMUM ANSWER: There are many apparent similarities of the controls, and that was originally designed into NIST 800-171 for a reason. Security controls are supposed to be reinforcing, and this control is only slightly different in its scope than others described earlier.

Control 3.1.6, is similar is reinforcing this control as well as others. The company's procedure guide can explicitly "rewrite" the original control description: "Prevent non-privileged users from executing privileged functions...." An example procedure write-up based upon the original control description is provided:

> EXAMPLE PROCEDURE: *Non-privileged users are prohibited from executing any privileged functions or system audits without the authority of the company's Chief Operating Officer, Chief Information Security Officer, or their designated representative. All requests will be submitted in writing with their first-line supervisor validating the need for such access for a limited and specified time.*

Additionally, this procedure limits higher-order (privileged) functions such as creating accounts for others, deleting database files, etc. It also requires the auditing of all privileged functions. It is suggested that the assigned SA at least weekly review and report inconsistencies of non-privileged/general users attempting (and, hopefully failing) to access parts of the internal infrastructure.

MORE COMPLETE ANSWER: A more thorough representation would be to provide copies of audit logs that include who, when, and what were the results of an audit evaluation; these artifacts should demonstrate that the company is following its internal cybersecurity procedures.

NOTE ABOUT "FREQUENCY": Many of the controls do not define how often a business should conduct a review, reassessment, etc. The business owner is afforded the opportunity to "define success" to the DOD Contract Officer or cybersecurity assessor. The important consideration is that the business determines frequency of reviews, in general, based upon the perceived or actual sensitivity of the data. This book will typically provide the more stringent DOD frequency standard, but nothing prevents a company from conducting less often reviews if it can be substantiated.

"Define your own success"

3.1.8 Limit unsuccessful logon attempts.
MINIMUM ANSWER: DOD standard policy is after three failed logons the system will automatically lock out the individual. Suggest this should be no more than five failed logons especially if employees are not computer savvy. This requires both the technical solution by the corporate IT system and described in the corporate procedure guide.

MORE COMPLETE ANSWER: For example, the additional ability to provide a screen capture that provides an artifact showing what happens when an employee reaches the maximum number of logons would meet this control; this could be added to the submission packet. It is also important to document procedures to include the process to regain network access.

3.1.9 Provide privacy and security notices consistent with applicable CUI rules.

MINIMUM ANSWER: Provided below is a current version of the **DOD Warning Banner** designed for company purposes. It should either be physically posted on or near each terminal or on the on-screen logon (preferred); this should also always include consent to monitoring. Recommend consulting with a legal representative for final approval and dissemination to employees.

[Company] Warning Banner

Use of this or any other [Company name] computer system constitutes consent to monitoring at all times.

This is a [Company name] computer system. All [Company name] computer systems and related equipment are intended for the communication, transmission, processing, and storage of official or other authorized information only. All [Company name] computer systems are subject to monitoring at all times to ensure proper functioning of equipment and systems including security devices and systems, to prevent unauthorized use and violations of statutes and security regulations, to deter criminal activity, and for other similar purposes. Any user of a [Company name] computer system should be aware that any information placed in the system is subject to monitoring and is not subject to any expectation of privacy.

If monitoring of this or any other [Company name] computer system reveals possible evidence of violation of criminal statutes, this evidence and any other related information, including identification information about the user, may be provided to law enforcement officials. If monitoring of this or any other [Company name] computer systems reveals violations of security regulations or unauthorized use, employees who violate security regulations or make unauthorized use of [Company name] computer systems are subject to appropriate disciplinary action.

Use of this or any other [Company name] *computer system constitutes consent to monitoring at all times.*

MORE COMPLETE ANSWER: Another consideration should be this policy also be coordinated with Human Resources (HR). This could further include that all employees sign a copy of this notice, and it be placed in their official file. Select and redacted copies could be used to demonstrate an active adherence to this requirement as a sampling provided to DOD. It could also potentially describe how the company has an ability to take actions against personnel who fail or violate this warning.

3.1.10. Use session lock with pattern-hiding displays to prevent access/viewing of data after period of inactivity.

MINIMUM ANSWER: While this may appear as solely a technical solution, it too should be identified in the company policy or procedure document. Session lock describes the period of inactivity when a computer terminal will automatically lock out the user. Suggest no more than 10 minutes for a computer lock out. Selecting longer is acceptable based upon many factors such as the type of work done (e.g., finance personnel) or the physical security level of the business (e.g., a restricted area with a limited number of authorized employees) is acceptable. However, be prepared to defend the balance between the company's need to meet DOD mission requirements and the risks of excessive session lock time outs.

Secondarily, **Pattern Hiding** is desired to prevent the concept of "shoulder surfing." Other like terms that are synonymous include **masking** and **obfuscation**.

Pattern hiding is designed to prevent an individual from observing an employee typing their password or Personal Identification Number (PIN). This control could include asterisks (*), for example, that mask the true information. This prevents insiders or even visitors from "stealing" another user's logon credentials.

Password without Pattern Hiding: PA$$w0rD
_____

Password with Pattern Hiding: ********
_____

Pattern Hiding

MORE COMPLETE ANSWER: The better solution could include much shorter periods for a time-out, and longer password length and complexity; DOD standard is at least 15 alpha-numeric and special characters.

- Alpha: abcde....
- Numeric: 12345...
- Special Characters:@ # $ % ....

(See Control 3.13.10 for a further discussion of **Multifactor Authentication (MFA)** and **Two Factor Authentication (2FA)).**

As an ongoing reminder, it is critical to place artifacts describing the technical solution demonstrated, for example, using a screen capture. It should be clear and easily traceable to this control's implementation by a DOD audit representative or assessor.

3.1.11. Terminate (automatically) a user session after a defined condition.

MINIMUM ANSWER: The simplest solution is a setting that the SA or other designated IT personnel, sets within the network's operating and management applications. Typically, most network operating systems can be set to enforce a terminal/complete lockout. This control implementation completely logs out the user and terminates any communications' sessions to include, for example, access to corporate databases, financial systems, or the Internet. It requires employees to re-initiate session connections to the network after this more complete session logout occurs.

MORE COMPLETE ANSWER: The complete answer could include screen captures of policy settings for session terminations and time-outs. The SA or designated company representative should be able to provide as an artifact.

3.1.12 Monitor and control remote access sessions.

MINIMUM ANSWER: This control is about remote access where one computer can control another computer over the Internet. This may include desktop support personnel "remoting into" an employee's computer to update the latest version of Firefox ® or a work-at-home employee inputting financial data into the corporate finance system. Identify these types of access as part of the procedural guide and describe who is authorized, how their access is limited (such as a finance employee can't issue themselves a corporate check), and the repercussions of violating the policy.

MORE COMPLETE ANSWER: The better technological approach could include restrictions to only IT help personnel using remote capabilities. Company policy should require regular review of auditable events and of logs. A screen capture would be helpful to show the policy settings specific to the remote desktop application.

3.1.13 Employ cryptographic mechanisms to protect the confidentiality of remote access sessions.

MINIMUM ANSWER: *This is a Data in Transit (DIT) issue*. Ensure the procedure requires the company's solution only uses approved cryptographic solutions. The **Advanced Encryption**

Standard (AES) is considered the current standard for encryption within DOD and the federal government. Also, use the 256 kilo-byte (kb) key length versions.

There are many commercial solutions in this area. Major software companies provide solutions that secure DIT and are typically at reasonable prices for small business options such as Symantec ®, McAfee ®, and Microsoft®.

---*Again, document, document, document*

MORE COMPLETE ANSWER: (See Control 3.1.3 for a more detailed representation). It's usually a capability directly afforded by the remote access application tool providers. The more critical issue within DOD is whether the application tool company ensures the application is coming from a US-based software developer.

There are many overseas developers, for example, to include Russia, former Warsaw Pact countries, and China, that are of concern to DOD. The apprehension is about commercial products from these nations and their potential threat to US national security. The business should confirm the product is coming from a current ally of the US; these would include the United Kingdom, Australia, etc. *Before purchasing, ensure you have done your homework, and provide proof the remote access software is accepted by DOD.*

3.1.14 Route remote access via managed access control points.
MINIMUM ANSWER: **Managed access control** points are about control of traffic through "trusted" connections. For example, this could be Verizon ® or AT&T® as the company's Internet Service Provider (ISP). It would be highly recommended to include any contracted services or Service Level Agreements (SLA) from these providers. They may include additional threat and spam filtering services that could reduce the "bad guys" from gaining access to corporate data; these are ideal artifacts for proof of satisfactorily meeting this control.

MORE COMPLETE ANSWER: Another addition could also be using what is called a **Virtual Private Network (VPN).** These are also common services the major providers have for additional costs.

Describing and providing such agreements to DOD could also identify a **defense in depth** approach; the first level is through the VPN service, and the second would be provided by the remote access software providing an additional layer of defense. Defense in depth can include such protective efforts to prevent unauthorized access to company IT assets:

- Physical protection (e.g., alarms, guards)
- Perimeter (e.g., firewalls, Intrusion Detection System (IDS), "Trusted Internet Connections")

- Application/Executables (e.g., **whitelisting** of authorized software, **blacklisting** blocking specified programs)
- Data (e.g., Data Loss Protection programs, Access controls, auditing)

3.1.15 Authorize remote execution of privileged commands and remote access to security-relevant information.

MINIMUM ANSWER: NIST 800-53 is the base document for all controls of NIST 800-171. It describes what businesses should manage and authorize privileged access for **security-relevant** information (e.g., finance information, IP, etc.), and using remote access only for "compelling operational needs."

This would specifically be documented in the restrictions of who and under what circumstances security-relevant information may be accessed be company personnel. The base NIST control requires the business to documents the rationale for this access in the System Security Plan (SSP); the interpretation is that the corporate cybersecurity policy should be an annex or appendix to the **SSP**. (See *System Security Plan (SSP) Template and Workbook: A Supplement to Understanding Your Responsibility to Meet NIST 800-171* on Amazon®)

MORE COMPLETE ANSWER: The ideal artifact suggested are the logs of remote access within and external to the company. This could also be found in the firewall audit logs as well as the remote access software application logs for comparison; these could also be used to identify log modifications that may be an indicator of **insider threat**. (See Control 3.2.3 for further discussion of this topic area).

3.1.16 Authorize wireless access prior to allowing such connections.

MINIMUM ANSWER: This would include wireless access agreements and more commonly described earlier is an Acceptable Use Policy (AUP). For example, an AUP would include defining the types and kinds of sites restricted from access by employees. These are typically gambling, pornography sites, etc. AUP's should be reviewed by a lawyer before requiring employees to sign.

MORE COMPLETE ANSWER: The more complete technical solution could identify unapproved sites and prevent "guest" access. (While guest access is not recommended, it is better to establish a secondary Wi-Fi network to accommodate and restrict visitors and third-party personnel from having direct access to the company network.)

It is also important that the Wi-Fi's network topology and encryption standard be provided as an artifact to DOD once the final packet is ready for submission. This should be part of the SSP and the corporate cybersecurity procedure document.

3.1.17 Protect wireless access using authentication and encryption.

MINIMUM ANSWER: Ensure this is included in the corporate procedure or policy that only authorized personnel within the firm have access and that the appropriate level of encryption is in place. Currently, the 802.11 standard is used and Wi-Fi Protected Access 2 (WPA2) encryption should be the minimum standard.

MORE COMPLETE ANSWER: Use of Wi-Fi "sniffing technology" while available may be prohibitively costly to smaller businesses. This technology can identify and audit unauthorized entry into the wireless portion of the network and subsequently provides access to the "physical" company network. Sniffers can be used to notify security personnel either through email or Short Message Service (SMS)-text alerts of such intrusions; if company data is highly sensitive, then this investment may be necessary. Also, maintain any documentation about the "sniffer" and its capabilities; provide it to DOD representatives as part of the official submission.

3.1.18. Control connection of mobile devices.

MINIMUM ANSWER: Most businesses' mobile devices are their cell phones. This would also include laptops and computer "pads" with web-enabled capabilities. This would first require as a matter of policy that employees only use of secure connections for their devices when not using the company's service provider—these should be verified as secure. This would also specifically bar employees use of unsecure Wi-fi **hot spots** such as fast food restaurants, coffee shops, etc. Home Wi-fi networks are typically secure but ensure that employees know to select **WPA2** as their standard at-home secure connection protocol.

MORE COMPLETE ANSWER: A better way to demonstrate this control is by discussing with the cell phone provider the ability to prevent corporate phones from using unsecure Wi-Fi networks at any time. The provider should be able to block access if the mobile phone does not "see" or recognize a secure connection. Include any proof from service agreements of such a provision as part of the submitted BOE.

3.1.19. Encrypt CUI on mobile devices.

MINIMUM ANSWER: The good news is that all the major carriers provide DAR encryption. Mobile phones typically can secure DAR on the phone behind a passcode, PIN, or even biometric capability such as fingerprint or facial recognition; these are acceptable by DOD standards. Check service agreements or add to the company's existing plan.

MORE COMPLETE ANSWER: There are several companies that provide proprietary and hardened devices for corporate users. These include state of the art encryption standards and further hardened phone bodies to prevent physical exploits of lost or stolen mobile devices. *Expect these solutions to be very expensive.*

3.1.20 Verify and control/limit connections to and use of external systems.

MINIMUM ANSWER: This control requires that all external or third-party connections to the company's network be verified. This would typically take the form of accepting another company (or even DOD agencies') Authority to Operate (ATO). This could be as simple as a memorandum, for example, recognizing another company's own self-assessment under NIST 800-171. It could also be accepting, through a process known as **reciprocity**, of accepting an ATO based upon NIST 800-53—more typical of DOD and other federal agencies. These are all legitimate means that are designed to ensure before a company allows another company to enter through its firewall (system security boundary) without some level of certainty that security was fully considered. Before an external system or network is allowed unfettered access within the corporations' data it is critical to identify the rules and restrictions for such access as part of this control.

As always, ensure procedures identify, and limit, such connections to only critical data feeds needed from third-parties to conduct formal business operations.

MORE COMPLETE ANSWER: This could include a request for ongoing scans of the external system and/or network every 30 days; this would be considered quite extreme, but dependent on data sensitivity. If sought, suggest that every six-months that the company receives copies of the anti-virus, anti-malware, and vulnerability patch scanning reports to identify current threats within the external system. This is designed to potentially address inbound threats and to enhance the company's overall security posture

3.1.21 Limit use of organizational portable storage devices on external systems.

MINIMUM ANSWER: This is not only about the use of USB thumb drives (see Chapter on Media Protection (MP)), it is also about external drives attached to a workstation or laptop, locally. While thumb drives are more capable to introduce malware and viruses to an unprotected network, external drives pose a real threat for data removal and theft. The company policy should include an approval process to "attach" only company provided drives and highly discourage personal devices attached by employees. Technical support should include the active scanning for viruses and malware every time the portable device is attached to the network.

MORE COMPLETE ANSWER: As discussed in more detail below regarding the use of thumb drives, IT personnel could disable at the **registry** anyone from using them. Where the need for external drives is necessitated, this control can be further enhanced through auditing of all such attachments and provide pre-formatted reports for company leadership. Auditing, as described under the AU control, should include capturing this activity.

3.1.22 Control CUI posted or processed on publicly accessible systems.

MINIMUM ANSWER: This addresses the control of publicly accessible information most commonly on the company's **public-facing** website. There needs to be procedural guidance and direction about who can release (usually public affairs office, etc.) and post information (usually webmaster, etc.) to the website. This should include a review of such data by personnel specifically trained to recognize CUI/CDI data. This may include information or data that discusses a company's current business relationship with the DOD, the activities it conducts, and the products and services its provides to both the public and private sector.

This should also address regular review of publicly accessible data, and the procedure to describe the process to remove unauthorized data if discovered.

MORE COMPLETE ANSWER: This could use automated scans of keywords and phrases that may alert audit personnel during their regular auditing activities. See the Auditing Control (AU) chapter. While this is a static means to alert untrained IT personnel, it could supplement that inadvertent release does not occur. Additional oversight should always be based upon the sensitivity of the information handled to not only include CUI/CDI, but Intellectual Property (IP) or other sensitive data, etc., that may harm the company if released into the public.

The decision process of how much encryption and added protection (such as hashing or emerging block chain encryption technologies) should be based on the risk to the system.

Consider the risk and the damage to the company if the data, CUI or not, is compromised

AWARENESS & TRAINING (AT)
A training program is a must

Awareness & Training is about an active cybersecurity training program for employees and a recurring education program that ensures their familiarity and compliance with protecting sensitive and CUI/CDI company data consistently. The websites (below) identify FREE government-sponsored sites a company can leverage without expending any of its own resources. The three major training requirements that can be expected of most vendors supporting federal government contract activities include:

1. **Cybersecurity Awareness Training.**
   https://securityawareness.usalearning.gov/cybersecurity/index.htm

2. **Insider Threat Training.**
   https://securityawareness.usalearning.gov/itawareness/index.htm
   (More discussion on the "Insider Threat" topic See Control 3.2.3).

3. **Privacy.** https://iatraining.disa.mil/eta/piiv2/launchPage.htm (This would specifically apply to any company that handles, processes or maintains Personally Identifiable Information (PII) and Personal Health Information (PHI). The author's expectation is that even though a company does not handle PII or PHI, the federal government to make this a universal training requirement.)

Defense Security Service (DSS) Cybersecurity Awareness Site

Basic Security Requirements:

3.2.1 Ensure that managers, systems administrators, and users of organizational information systems are made aware of the security risks associated with their activities and of the applicable policies, standards, and procedures related to the security of organizational information systems.

MINIMUM ANSWER: *Human beings are the weakest link in the cybersecurity "war."* The greatest threat is from the employee who unwittingly selects a link that allows an intrusion into the corporate system, or worse, those who maliciously remove, modify, or delete sensitive CUI/CDI.

The answer should be documented regarding initial and annual refresher training requirements for everyone in the company; not just average employees but **must** *include* senior managers and support subcontractors. Provide a sampling of select employees that have taken training, and ensuring it is current within the past year.

MORE COMPLETE ANSWER: A possible demonstration of more complete solution is within the policy specific direction to IT support personnel. There could be a system notification that allows them after notification, manually or by automated means, to *suspend* access until training is completed. Strong documentation is important specific to awareness training.

3.2.2 Ensure that organizational personnel are adequately trained to carry out their assigned information security-related duties and responsibilities.

MINIMUM ANSWER: This is not only required awareness training, but also specialized training for privileged users. This is usually Operating System (OS) training specific to the company's architecture. It is possible to have multiple OS's. Privileged users are only required to show, for example, some form of training certificate, to meet this requirement. All IT personnel who have elevated privileges *must* have such training before they are authorized to execute their duties.

Additionally, if the company uses Microsoft ® or Linux ® Operating Systems, privileged users will have some level of certification to show a familiarity with these programs. This could include major national certifications for these applications or basic familiarity courses from free training sites, for example, Khan Academy® (https://www.khanacademy.org/) or Udacity® (https://www.udacity.com/).

DOD has not clearly defined the level and type of training for this requirement. It requires privileged users to have an understanding and training certificate (with no specified time length) for the major Operating System (OS) the corporate IT infrastructure employs.

MORE COMPLETE ANSWER: If IT personnel have formal certification (such as from a Microsoft ®
partner training program), these are ideal artifacts that should be part of the BOE.

Derived Security Requirements:

3.2.3 Provide security awareness training on recognizing and reporting potential indicators of insider threat.

MINIMUM ANSWER: The DOD's Defense Security Service (DSS) in Quantico, VA, is the executive
agent for insider threat activities. The DSS provides many training opportunities and toolkits on
Insider Threat. These are available from their agency website for free at
http://www.dss.mil/it/index.html. This is an excellent resource to create an insider threat
training program already developed for the company's use.

Document company minimum training requirements for both general and privileged users such
as watching select online instruction or computer-based training opportunities from DSS.
Everyone in the company should participate and satisfactorily complete the training.

MORE COMPLETE ANSWER: More complete proof of company compliance with this security
control requirement might include guest speakers or insider threat brown-bag events around

lunch time. Company training personnel should capture attendance records to include sign-in rosters. These could be used for annual training requirements specific to insider threat familiarity.

Also, recommend a **train-the-trainer program** where select individuals are trained by either DSS or other competent company that become corporate resources. These assigned individuals could provide both training and first-responder support as needed, and be deployed to other company sites.

AUDIT AND ACCOUNTABILITY (AU)
System Logs and their Regular Review

The AU control is primarily about the ability of the system owner/company to monitor unauthorized access to the system through system logging functions of the Operating System and other network devices such as firewalls. A SA is typically assigned the duty to review log files; these may include both authorized and unauthorized access to the network, applications, databases, financial systems, etc. Most businesses will rely on manual review; however, some "smart" servers and firewalls can provide automated alerts to IT personnel of unauthorized use or intrusion. The key is to understand the auditing capabilities of the corporate system and be prepared to defend its capabilities and limitations if DOD representatives or third-party DOD assessors request proof of control compliance.

```
usion Detection System

.**] [1:1407:9] SNMP trap udp [**]
[Classification: Attempted Information Leak] [Priority: 2]
03/06-8:14:09.082119 192.168.1.167:1052 -> 172.30.128.27:162
UDP TTL:118 TOS:0x0 ID:29101 IpLen:20 DgmLen:87

Personal Firewall

3/6/2006 8:14:07 AM,"Rule ""Block Windows File Sharing"" blocked (192.168.1.54,
netbios-ssn(139)).","Rule ""Block Windows File Sharing"" blocked (192.168.1.54,
netbios-ssn(139)). Inbound TCP connection. Local address,service is
(KENT(172.30.128.27),netbios-ssn(139)). Remote address,service is
(192.168.1.54,39922). Process name is ""System""."

3/3/2006 9:04:04 AM,Firewall configuration updated: 398 rules.,Firewall configuration
updated: 398 rules.

Antivirus Software, Log 1

3/4/2006 9:33:50 AM,Definition File Download,KENT,userk,Definition downloader
3/4/2006 9:33:09 AM,AntiVirus Startup,KENT,userk,System
3/3/2006 3:56:46 PM,AntiVirus Shutdown,KENT,userk,System

Antivirus Software, Log 2

240203071234,16,3,7,KENT,userk,,,,,,16777216,"Virus definitions are
current.",0,,0,,,,,0,,,,,,,,,SAVPROD,{ xxxxxxxx-xxxx-xxxx-xxxx-xxxxxxxxxxxx },End
User,(IP)-192.168.1.121,,GROUP,0:0:0:0:0:0,9.0.0.338,,,,,,,,,,,,,,

Antispyware Software

DSO Exploit: Data source object exploit (Registry change, nothing done)  HKEY_USERS\S-
1-5-19\Software\Microsoft\Windows\CurrentVersion\Internet Settings\Zones\0\1004!=W=?
```

Audit log type examples. The logs above are good examples of the system logs that should be reviewed regularly. These are the business's responsibility to monitor the network actively. Another term of high interest is **Continuous Monitoring (ConMon);** see the article at Appendix C discussing the importance of ConMon capabilities. ConMon can be accomplished by both manual and automated means, and auditing is a major control family supporting the objectives of this cybersecurity principle.

ConMon activities are best described as the ability of the business to "continuously" monitor the state of its network within its defined security boundary. It should be a capability to determine, for example, who, when, and what are within the company's security boundary and any reporting requirements in the event of an intrusion. It will be based on log discovery of especially unauthorized activities.
(SOURCE: *Guide to Computer Security Log Management*, NIST SP 800-92, September 2006, http://nvlpubs.nist.gov/nistpubs/Legacy/SP/nistspecialpublication800-92.pdf) .

For a greater description about the purpose and components of Continuous Monitoring see Appendix C: *Continuous Monitoring: A More Detailed Discussion.*

Basic Security Requirements:

3.3.1 Create, protect, and retain information system audit records to the extent needed to enable the monitoring, analysis, investigation, and reporting of unlawful, unauthorized, or inappropriate information system activity.

MINIMUM ANSWER: The key part of this control is about audit record retention. The control defines the **retention period** as a vague capability to retain such records to the greatest "extent possible." The guidance should always be based upon the sensitivity of the data. Another consideration should include the ability to provide forensic data to investigators to determine the intrusion over a period.

The historical OPM Breach occurred over several years until OPM even recognized multiple incidents. This included the exfiltration of millions of personnel and security background investigation files. OPM failures while numerous, included poor audit processes and review as a major factor in the success of nation-state hackers. OPM's poor audit and retention processes made reconstructing critical events more than difficult for government forensics and associated criminal investigations.

The recommendation to small and medium businesses conducting DOD contract activities would be at least 1 year and preferably 2 years of audit log retention. Companies should regularly discuss with DOD its specified requirements and should also visit the National Archives Record Agency (NARA) (www.nara.gov) for CUI/CDI data retention as part of an active audit program.

Businesses should balance operations (and long-term costs) with security (the ability to reconstruct an intrusion to support law enforcement)

MORE COMPLETE ANSWER: A greater ability to recognize breaches (events and incidents) could include an additional internal process and assigned first-responders who would act upon these occurrences. This response team may have additional specialized training to include use of select network analysis support tools to include **packet inspection** training using tools such as Wireshark ® (https://www.wireshark.org/).

3.3.2 Ensure that the actions of individual information system users can be uniquely traced to those users, so they can be held accountable for their actions.

MINIMUM ANSWER: This is about that capture of individual users as they access the system. Access logs should include, for example, user identification information, timestamps of all access, databases or applications accessed, and number of failed logon attempts. This control is designed for potential forensic reconstruction for either internal policy violations or external threat intrusions. Any policy considerations should include at least weekly review, but any audit review periodicity should be based on the sensitivity and criticality of data to the business's overall mission.

MORE COMPLETE ANSWER: A more complete means to address this control is using automated alerts to key IT and management personnel. This could include capabilities from existing "smart" firewalls or more advanced solutions may include a **Security Information & Event Management (SIEM)** solution. These are more complicated and expensive solutions, but current developments employing modern Artificial Intelligence and Machine Learning technologies to more proactively identify threats is evolving rapidly; these solutions should be less expensive and easier to deploy within the next decade.

Derived Security Requirements:

3.3.3 Review and update audited events.

MINIMUM ANSWER: This is a similar requirement to other AU controls above to regularly review audit logs. We recommend at least weekly reviews.

MORE COMPLETE ANSWER: To more completely address this control, IT personnel could categorize the log types being collected. These could include, for example, Operating System (OS) (network), application, firewall, database logs, etc.

3.3.4 Alert in the event of an audit process failure.

MINIMUM ANSWER: This is an active ability developed within the company's audit technology that can alert personnel of an audit failure.

This could include local alarms, flashing lights, SMS, and email alerts to key company personnel. This will require SA and IT personnel to set policy settings to be established as part of the normal checks in support of the overall audit function and control. A description of the technical implementation and immediate actions to be taken by personnel should be identified. This should include activation of the Incident Response (IR) Plan.

MORE COMPLETE ANSWER: Additional technical solutions could include supplementary systems to be monitored. This could include the state of all audit-capable devices and functions. This may also include a separate computer or a backup auditing server for the storage of logs not on the primary system; this would prevent intruders from deleting or changing logs to hide their presence in the network.

These solutions will ultimately add additional complexity and cost. Ensure any solution is supportable both financially and technically by company decision-makers. While to have greater security is an overall desire of the NIST 800-171 implementation, it should be balanced with a practical and measurable value-added approach to adding any new technologies. It should also be a further consideration that the incorporation of new technologies should address the impacts of added complexity and determining the ability of IT support personnel to maintain it.

3.3.5 Correlate audit review, analysis, and reporting processes for investigation and response to indications of inappropriate, suspicious, or unusual activity.

MINIMUM ANSWER: This should identify the technical actions taken by authorized audit personnel to pursue when analyzing suspicious activity on the network.

It should also be tied to the IR Plan, and be tested at least annually. (See Control IR for further discussion of **DOD Precedence Identification** and determine actions based on the level of severity).

MORE COMPLETE ANSWER: See Control 3.3.2 for a more detailed discussion of employing a SIEM solution. In addition to manual analysis, the company could leverage the capabilities of newer threat identification technologies such as SIEM and "smart" Intrusion Detection and Prevention devices.

3.3.6 Provide audit reduction and report generation to support on-demand analysis and reporting.

MINIMUM ANSWER: Audit reduction provides for "on-demand" audit review, analysis, and reporting requirements.

This should at least use manual methods to collect audits from across multiple audit logging devices to assist in potential forensic needs. Any procedural effort to support audit reduction most likely can use commercial support applications and scripts (small programs typically written specific to the business's unique IT environment) that IT personnel should be able to assist in their identification, development and procurement.

MORE COMPLETE ANSWER: IT personnel could identify more automated and integrated audit reduction solutions. Likely candidates could be "smart" firewalls or Security Information and Event Management (SIEM) solutions.

3.3.7 Provide an information system capability that compares and synchronizes internal system clocks with an authoritative source to generate time stamps for audit records.

MINIMUM ANSWER: The simplest answer is to have IT personnel use the Network Time Protocol (NTP) on **NTP port 123** to provide US Naval Observatory timestamps as the standard for the network. This is used as the authoritative source within DOD. The system clocks of all processors (computers, firewalls, etc.) within the company should be set to the exact same time when first initialized by IT support staffs; this should be an explicit policy requirement.

It is suggested that SA personnel review and compare the external (NTP server time stamp) with internal system clocks. This can be used to identify log changes if synchronization is not the same from the external and internal clock settings. Log changes may be an indicator of unauthorized access and manipulation of log files by hackers.

MORE COMPLETE ANSWER: There are several automated programs that can be used, and good basic programmers within the company could write **scripts** (small pieces of executable code) to provide these comparisons more easily.

3.3.8 Protect audit information and audit tools from unauthorized access, modification, and deletion.

MINIMUM ANSWER: This control requires a greater protection of audit files and auditing tools from unauthorized users. These tools can be exploited by intruders to change log files or delete them entirely to hide their entry into the system. Password protect and limit use to only authorized personnel. Document this process accordingly.

MORE COMPLETE ANSWER: This information could be stored in some other server not part of the normal audit log capture area. Additionally, conduct regular backups to prevent intruders from manipulating logs; this will allow a means to compare changes, and identify potential incidents in the network for action by senior management or law enforcement.

3.3.9 Limit management of audit functionality to a subset of privileged users.

MINIMUM ANSWER: See Control 3.3.8 for reducing the numbers of personnel with access to audit logs and functions. Maintaining a roster of personnel with appropriate user agreements can afford the ability to limit personnel as well as provide value in any future forensic activities required.

MORE COMPLETE ANSWER: There are several products such as CyberArk ® that could be used to manage and monitor privileged user access to audit information. This product will be a relatively expensive solution for small and some medium-sized businesses.

CONFIGURATION MANAGEMENT (CM)
The True Foundation of Cybersecurity

The real importance of Configuration Management is it is in fact the "opposite side of the same coin" called **cybersecurity**. CM is used to track and confirm changes to the system's baseline; this could be changes in hardware, firmware, and software that would alert IT professionals to unauthorized changes to the IT environment. CM is used to confirm, and ensure programmatic controls prevent changes that have not been adequately tested or approved.

CM requires establishing baselines for tracking, controlling, and managing a business's internal IT infrastructure specific to NIST 800-171. Companies with an effective CM process need to consider information security implications with respect to the development and operation of information systems. This will include the active management of changes to company hardware, software, and documentation.

Effective CM of information systems requires the integration of the management of secure configurations into the CM process. If good CM exists as a well-defined "change" process, protection of the IT environment is more assured. This should be considered as the second most important security control. It is suggested that both management and IT personnel have adequate knowledge and training to maintain this process since it is so integral to good programmatic and cybersecurity practice.

Basic Security Requirements:

3.4.1 Establish and maintain baseline configurations and inventories of organizational information systems (including hardware, software, firmware, and documentation) throughout the respective system development life cycles.

MINIMUM ANSWER: This control can be best met by hardware, software, and firmware (should be combined with hardware) listings; these are the classic artifacts required for any system within the DOD. Updating these documents as changes to the IT architecture is both a critical IT and logistics' functions. Ensure these staffs are well-coordinated about system changes. ***This should be included in the System Security Plan (SSP).***

Also, NIST 800-171 requires document control of all reports, documents, manuals, etc. The currency of all related documents should be managed in a centralized repository.

Where documents may be sensitive, such as describing existing weaknesses or vulnerabilities of the IT infrastructure, these documents should have a greater level of control. The rationale for greater control of such documents is if these documents were "found" in the public, hackers or

Advanced Persistent Threats (i.e., adversarial nation-states) could use to this information to conduct exploits. Vulnerabilities about company systems should be marked and controlled at least at the CUI/CDI level.

MORE COMPLETE ANSWER: Suggested better approaches to exercising good **version control** activities would be using a shared network drive, or a more advance solution could use Microsoft ® SharePoint ®. An active version control tool should only allow authorized personnel to make changes to key documents and system changes and their associated **versioning**—major changes within the IT architecture, for example, from version 2.0 to 3.0. This should also maintain audit records of who and when a file is accessed and modified.

3.4.2 Establish and enforce security configuration settings for information technology products employed in organizational information systems.

MINIMUM/MORE COMPLETE ANSWER: There should be an identification of any security configuration settings in business's procedural documents. This would include technical policy settings, for example, number of failed logons, minimum password length, mandatory logoff settings, etc. These settings should be identified by a company's Operating System, software application or program.

Derived Security Requirements:

3.4.3 Track, review, approve/disapprove, and audit changes to information systems.

MINIMUM ANSWER: This control addresses a defined corporate change *process*. This should be able to add or remove IT components within the network and provide needed currency regarding the state of the network. This should not be a purely IT staff function. If the firm can afford additional infrastructure personnel, it should assign a configuration manager; this person would administer the CM process.

MORE COMPLETE ANSWER: This could use Commercial Off the Shelf Technologies (COTS) that could be used to establish a more sophisticated CM database. This could also afford a more capable audit ability to prevent unauthorized changes.

3.4.4 Analyze the security impact of changes prior to implementation.

MINIMUM ANSWER: Under DOD's risk management process, it requires that any changes to the baseline necessitates some level of technical analysis. This analysis is described as a **Security Impact Analysis (SIA),** and it is looking for any positive or negative changes that are considered **security relevant**.

This analysis should look at any change to the architecture, be it changes in hardware, software, firmware, or architecture. This should be described in the corporate CM process and could be as basic as a write-up from a member of the IT team, for example, that the change will or will not have a security impact, and it may or may not be security relevant.

If the change introduces a "negative" impact, such as eliminating backup capabilities or introducing currently unsupportable software (possibly due to funding constraints), *it is the responsibility of the company to reinitiate the NIST 800-171 process in-full and advise DOD of the rationale for change.*

See CM control 3.4.4 for a detailed Decision-tree.

MORE COMPLETE ANSWER: A more complete solution to this control would include, for example, the addition of a new software product that supports vulnerability scans using corporate anti-virus and malware applications or software products. Attach these reports as part of the record.

In the case of hardware updates, the company could demonstrate its SCRM process by attaching proof that the manufacturer is an authorized vendor approved by the DOD. Access to DOD's Approved Products List (APL) may require the Contracting Officer Representative (COR) or Contracting Officer (CO) to approve access to DOD databases maintained by the Defense Information Systems Agency (DISA) at Fort Meade, MD. It most likely will only allow a limited number of company personnel to be issued DOD CAC "tokens" to access these sites; the positive review of these databases will demonstrate the proper level of due diligence for any current or future Authorization to Operate (ATO).

3.4.5 Define, document, approve, and enforce physical and logical access restrictions associated with changes to the information system.

MINIMUM/MORE COMPLETE ANSWER: "Access restrictions" are aligned with the earlier discussed AC controls. As part of a corporate CM policy, any changes to the IT baseline needs to be captured within a formal process, approved by that process, and documented. Documentation is typically maintained in a CM database, and more specifically, it would require the update of any hardware or software lists. Proof of compliance would be the production of updated listings that are maintained by the CM database. This should include the updating of any network diagrams describing in a graphic form a description of the corporate network; these are all explicit requirements under NIST 800-171. These artifacts should also be included in the **SSP**.

3.4.6 Employ the principle of least functionality by configuring the information system to provide only essential capabilities.

MINIMUM ANSWER: The DOD has defined the use, for example, of File Transfer Protocol (FTP), Bluetooth, or peer-to-peer networking as unsecure protocols. These protocols are unauthorized within DOD environments, and companies seeking NIST 800-171 approval are best to follow this direction as well. Any written procedure should attempt to at least annually reassess whether a determination of the security of all functions, ports, protocols, or services are still correct.

MORE COMPLETE ANSWER: The use of automated network packet tools is recommended to conduct such reassessments. Ensure that IT personnel have the right experience and skill to provide good analysis of this control requirement.

3.4.7 Restrict, disable, and prevent the use of nonessential programs, functions, ports, protocols, and services.

MINIMUM ANSWER: Nonessential programs, functions, ports and protocols are prime attack avenues for would-be hackers. Any programs that are not used for the conduct of business operations should be removed. Where that is not possible, these programs should be blacklisted to run in the company's IT environment. (See 3.4.8. below).

In terms of ports and protocols, this will require IT staff direct involvement in the decision-making process. Certain ports are typically needed for any 21st Century company's daily operation. For example, ports 80, 8080, and 443 are used to send HTTP (web traffic); these ports will typically be required to be active.

Port Number	Application Supported
20	File Transport Protocol (FTP) Data
23	Telnet
25	Simple Mail Transfer Protocol (SMTP)
80, 8080, 443	Hypertext Transport Protocol (HTTP) → WWW
110	Post Office Protocol version 3 (POP3)

Common Ports and Their Associated Protocols

For those ports and protocols that are not required, they should be closed by designated IT personnel. This prevents hackers from exploiting open entries into the corporate infrastructure. Ensure a copy of all open and closed ports is readily available to DOD representatives for review as part of the NIST 800-171 requirements.

MORE COMPLETE ANSWER: The business could employ tools that check for unused and open ports. This could include regular reassessment of whether ports need to remain active. As mentioned earlier, products such as Wireshark ® could be used as a low-cost solution to conduct any reassessment of the corporate infrastructure.

3.4.8 Apply deny-by-exception (blacklist) policy to prevent the use of unauthorized software or deny all, permit-by-exception (whitelisting) policy to allow the execution of authorized software.

MINIMUM/MORE COMPLETE ANSWER: The company should employ **blacklisting** or **whitelisting,** (See Control 3.14.2 for more information), to prohibit the execution of unauthorized software programs or applications within the information system. A copy of the current listing should be part of the formal Body of Evidence (BOE).

3.4.9 Control and monitor user-installed software.

MINIMUM ANSWER: The policy should always be that only authorized administrators, such as designated SA's and senior help desk personnel, be allowed to add or delete software from user computers.

There should also be a defined process to request specialized software be added for unique users. These may include finance personnel, architects, statisticians, etc. that require specialized stand-alone software that may or may not connect to the Internet.

MORE COMPLETE ANSWER: This could include as part of the company's normal audit process the review of whether personnel are adding software and bypassing security measures (such as getting passwords from IT authorized individuals). This may also be addressed in the AUP and supported by appropriate HR activities that can be pursued against individuals of any such violations.

IDENTIFICATION AND AUTHENTICATION (IA)

Why two-factor authentication is so important?

The 2015 Office of Personnel Management (OPM) breach could have been prevented if this control family was properly implemented and enforced. The one positive effect that the OPM breach produced for DOD and other federal agencies was the explicit requirement from Congress that these requirements became mandatory. Congress's focus on the use of Two-Factor Authentication (2FA) and Multi-Factor Authentication (MFA) has provided positive results for the federal government and impetus for more stringent cybersecurity measures beyond the government's IT boundaries.

While some businesses will be afforded, for example, Common Access Cards (CAC) to accomplish 2FA between the company and DOD, most won't be authorized such access. Implementation will require various levels of investment, and the use of 2FA devices, or also called "tokens." This too will require additional financial costs and technical integration challenges for the average business.

For many small businesses, this will require some sizeable investment on the part of the company and a clear commitment to working with the DOD. Solutions could include, for example, RSA® tokens—these are small devices that constantly rotate a security variable (a key) that a user enters in addition to a password or Personal Identification Number (PIN). This solution affords one potential solution to businesses to meet the 2FA requirement.

According to The House Committee on Oversight and Government Reform report on September 7th, 2016, OPM's leadership failed to "implement basic cyber hygiene, such as maintaining current authorities to operate <u>and employing strong multi-factor authentication</u>, despite years of warning from the Inspector General… tools were available that could have prevented the breaches…" (SOURCE: <u>https://oversight.house.gov/wp-content/uploads/2016/09/The-OPM-Data-Breach-How-the-Government-Jeopardized-Our-National-Security-for-More-than-a-Generation.pdf</u>)

The best approaches will require good market surveys of the available resources and be mindful that two-factor does not just need to be a card or token solution. Other options would include biometrics (fingerprints, facial recognition, etc.) or Short Message Service (SMS) 2FA solution as used by Amazon® to verify its customers. They use a Two-Step verification process that provides a "verification code sent to the customers personal cell phone or home phone to verify their identity.

Be prepared to do serious "homework" on these controls, and research all potential solutions. Once this control is resolved, the company will be in a better position not just with DOD but have serious answers that will ensure protection of its sensitive data.

Basic Security Requirements:

3.5.1 Identify information system users, processes acting on behalf of users, or devices.

MINIMUM/MORE COMPLETE ANSWER: This control should identify/reference current business procedures as outlined in the **AU** control above. It should address that audit is used to identify system users, the processes (applications) and the devices (computers) accessed.

3.5.2 Authenticate (or verify) the identities of those users, processes, or devices, as a prerequisite to allowing access to organizational information systems.

MINIMUM ANSWER: While basic logon and password information could be used, Control 3.5.3 below, requires Multifactor or Two-factor Authentication (2FA). DOD requires 2FA, and NIST 800-171 requires it.

Remember, if the company is not immediately prepared to execute a 2FA solution, *a POAM is required*.

MORE COMPLETE ANSWER: The better answer is the employment of some form of 2FA. It could be a **hard token** solution such as a CAC or PIV card. The other option would include such virtual solutions that would use email or SMS messaging like Google ® or Amazon ® to provide 2FA; this **soft token** solution is typically easier and less expensive to deploy. It can be more easily deployed to meet this DOD and NIST 800-171 requirement.

Derived Security Requirements:

3.5.3 Use multifactor authentication for local and network access to privileged accounts and for network access to non-privileged accounts.

MINIMUM ANSWER: See Control 3.5.2 above. Ensure the requirement for MFA or 2FA are part of the company's cybersecurity policy/procedure.

MORE COMPLETE ANSWER: (See Control 3.5.2 for suggested approaches).

3.5.4 Employ replay-resistant authentication mechanisms for network access to privileged and nonprivileged accounts.

MINIMUM ANSWER: This control requires replay-resistant technologies to prevent replay attacks. **Replay attacks** are also known as a **playback attack**. This is an attack where the hacker captures legitimate traffic from an authorized user, and presumably a positively identified network user, and uses it to gain unauthorized access to a network. This is also considered a form of a **Man-in-the-Middle** type attack.

The easiest solution to resolving this control is to have company IT personnel disable **Secure Socket Layer (SSL)**—which DOD no longer authorizes. Businesses should use the **Transport Layer Security (TLS) 2.0** or higher; it as a required DOD standard.

If the business needs to continue the use of SSL to maintain connectivity with, for example, external or third-party data providers, a POAM is required. Efforts should be made to discuss with these data providers when they will no longer be using SSL. This discussion should begin as soon as possible to advise DOD through a POAM that demonstrates the company is conducting its proper due diligence to protect its CUI/CDI.

MORE COMPLETE ANSWER: A potentially expensive solution could include the addition of a **SIEM** solution. There are many major IT network providers that have added artificial intelligence capabilities to better detect this type of attack; identify any solution carefully.

3.5.5 Prevent reuse of identifiers for a defined period.

MINIMUM ANSWER: This IA control directs that "individual, group, role, or device identifiers" from being reused. This should be included as part of any written procedure and defined in system policies to prevent identifiers from being reused. This could include email address names (individual), administrator accounts (group), or device identifiers such as "finan_db" designating a high value target such as a "financial database" (device).

The reason for this control is to prevent intruders who have gained information about such identifiers having less of a capability to use this information for an exploit of the business. This will help better thwart hacker's intelligence collection and analysis of a company's internal network. This control is designed to prevent intruders' abilities to gain access to corporate systems and their resident CUI/CDI repositories.

MORE COMPLETE ANSWER: Reuse of individual identifiers should be discouraged, for example, in the case of a returning employee. This is a basic suggestion: 'John.Smith@cui-company.com' could be varied to example, 'John.H.Smith2@cui-company.com.

3.5.6 Disable identifiers after a defined period of inactivity.

MINIMUM/MORE COMPLETE ANSWER: This requires that after a defined time-out setting, the system terminates its connection. The recommendation is 30 minutes maximum, but as mentioned earlier, the time-out should always be based on the data sensitivity.

3.5.7 Enforce a minimum password complexity and change of characters when new passwords are created.

MINIMUM ANSWER: If using passwords for authentication purposes, the expectation is that a POAM has been developed until such time a 2FA or MFA solution is in place. The standard complexity is supposed to be at least 15 characters that include at least 2 or more alpha, numeric, and special characters to reduce the likelihood of compromise.

MORE COMPLETE ANSWER: Increased length and variability can be enforced by automated policy settings of the network. Another suggestion is to use passphrases. These can be harder to "crack" by normal hacking tools and are typically easier for users to memorize.

The best solutions are still 2FA or MFA

The factors:

1. Something you know (e.g., password/PIN)
2. Something you have (e.g., cryptographic identification device, token)
3. Something you are (e.g., biometric: fingerprint, iris, etc.).

3.5.8 Prohibit password reuse for a specified number of generations.

MINIMUM ANSWER: This is usually set by policy and the designated SA's that limit the number of times a password can be reused; *passwords within DOD are required to be changed every 90 days.* This function should be automated by authorized IT personnel. Suggested reuse of a prior password should be at least 10 or greater

MORE COMPLETE ANSWER: Technical settings can be established for *no* reuse. This ensures that hackers who may have exploited one of the user's other business or even (and more especially) personal accounts, can less likely to be effective against corporate computer networks and assets.

3.5.9 Allow temporary password use for system logons with an immediate change to a permanent password.

MINIMUM/MORE COMPLETE ANSWER: This setting is typically built into normal network operating systems. This requirement for users should be appropriately included in the recommended procedure guide.

3.5.10 Store and transmit only encrypted representation of passwords.

MINIMUM ANSWER: This is both a DIT and DAR issue, See Control 3.1.3 for a conceptual diagram. IT personnel should be regularly verifying that password data stores are always encrypted.

This control requires that all passwords are encrypted and approved by NIST's sanctioned process under FIPS 140-2. See Control 3.13.11 for the NIST website to confirm whether a cryptographic solution is approved.

MORE COMPLETE ANSWER: Suggested greater protections could require encrypted passwords are not collocated on the same main application or database server that stores major portions of the business's data repository. A separate server (physical or virtual) could prevent hacker exploits from accessing company data stores.

3.5.11. Obscure feedback of authentication information.

MINIMUM/MORE COMPLETE ANSWER: This is like **pattern hiding** as described in Control 3.1.10. The system should prevent unauthorized individuals from compromising system-level authentication by inadvertently observing in-person ("shoulder surfing") or virtually (by viewing password entries by privileged users) remotely. It relies upon obscuring the "feedback of authentication information", for example, displaying asterisks (*) or hash symbols (#) when a user types their password. This setting should be enforced automatically and prevent general users from changing this setting.

INCIDENT RESPONSE (IR)
What do you do when you're attacked?

Incident Response (IR) primarily requires a plan, an identification of who or what agency is notified when a breach has occurred, and a testing of the plan over time. This control requires the development of an Incident Response Plan (IRP). There are many templates available online, and if there is an existing relationship with a DOD agency, companies should be able to get an agency specific template.

EVENT (less defined/initial occurrence) → **INCIDENT** (defined/confirmed/high impact)

Incident Response Spectrum

The first effort should be identifying with DOD representatives what constitutes a reportable **event** that formally becomes an **incident**. This could include a confirmed breach that has occurred to the IT infrastructure. Incidents could include anything from a Denial of Service (DOS) attack—an overloading of outwardly facing web or mail servers--, or an exfiltration of data—where CUI/CDI and corporate data has been copied or moved to outside of the company's firewall/perimeter. Incidents could also include destruction of data that the company's IT staff, for example, identifies through ongoing audit activities.

Secondarily, who do you notify? Do you alert your assigned Contract Officer Representative (COR), the Contract Office, DOD's US Cybercommand at Fort Meade, MD, or possibly the Department of Homeland Security's (DHS) Computer Emergency Response Team (CERT) (https://www.us-cert.gov/forms/report) ? Company representatives will have to ask their assigned COR where to file standard DOD "incident" reports. They should be able to provide templates and forms specific to the DOD agency.

Finally, this security control will require testing at least *annually*, but more often is recommended. Until comfortable with the IR "reporting chain," ***practice, practice, practice***.

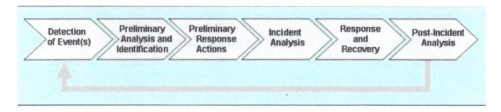

Cyber Incident Life Cycle. This diagram will assist in approaching the IR activity, and will better assist in coordination with DOD cybersecurity incident response organizations. Recognizing this as either an "event" (not necessarily a negative occurrence) versus an "incident" is an internal call by the company's leadership in coordination with its own security and IT professional staffs. An incident specifically requires alerting DOD as soon as the intrusion is *recognized*.

Verify with the respective DOD agency its reporting standards. Typically, **events** need to be reported within 24 hours upon recognition, and **incidents** immediately upon recognition. Always verify this with the assigned COR.

The chart below categorizes current DOD precedence.

Precedence	Category	Description
0	0	Training and Exercises
1	1	Root Level Intrusion (Incident)
2	2	User Level Intrusion (Incident)
3	4	Denial of Service (Incident)
4	7	Malicious Logic (Incident)
5	3	Unsuccessful Activity Attempt (Event)
6	5	Non-Compliance Activity (Event)
7	6	Reconnaissance (Event)
8	8	Investigating (Event)
9	9	Explained Anomaly (Event)

DOD Precedence Categorization. Nine (9) is the lowest event where little is known, and IT personnel are attempting to determine whether this activity should be elevated to alert company leadership or to "close it out." One (1) is a deep attack. It identifies that the incident has gained "root" access. This level of incident is critical since an intruder has nearly unlimited access to the network and its data. (SOURCE: CYBER INCIDENT HANDLING PROGRAM, CJCSM 6510.01B, 18 December 2014, http://www.jcs.mil/Portals/36/Documents/Library/Manuals/m651001.pdf?ver=2016-02-05-175710-897)

Basic Security Requirements:

3.6.1 Establish an operational incident-handling capability for organizational information systems that includes adequate preparation, detection, analysis, containment, recovery, and user response activities.

MINIMUM ANSWER: This control addresses a "capability" that needs to be established to respond to events and incidents within the firm's IT security boundary.

This should include the **People, Process and Technology (PPT) Model** as a recommended guide for answering many of the controls within NIST 800-171. While solutions will not necessarily require a **technological** answer, consideration of the **people** (e.g., who? what skill sets? etc.) and **process** (e.g., notifications to senior management, action workflows, etc.) will meet many of the response requirements.

Use the **Cyber Incident Life Cycle** above to guide the company's operational incident-handling artifact/procedure. This should be an annex to the SSP. (See *System Security Plan (SSP) Template and Workbook: A Supplement to Understanding Your Responsibility to Meet NIST 800-171* on Amazon®). **The PPT Model** can be used to guide and formulate the IRP annex. A suggested approach is described below, and includes the kinds of questions that should be answered to best demonstrate how best to formulate a good IRP:

- Preparation

    o People: Who will perform the action or activity? Training needed? Skill sets?
    o Process: Training policies for cybersecurity and IT professionals to support the IRP
    o Technology: What technology already exists to support IR? What technologies are needed?

- Detection

    o People: Are IT staff able to use audit tools properly to detect intrusions?
    o Process: What are 'best practice' approaches to detect intrusions? Monitor firewall logs? Monitor user activity?
    o Technology: Is the technology's data library current? Are automatic updates enabled?

- Analysis

    o People: Are IT staff capable to do the analysis required? Can they determine false positive activity?

- Process: What is the process leadership wants to get effective and actionable data from IT staff? What are the demands for immediate and final reporting timelines?
- Technology: Are the right tools on-site? Can open source/web solutions useful? Can DOD or DHS provide helpful data feeds to remain current of threats?

- Containment

  - People: Can IT staff stop the ongoing attack? Do they require additional coding scripting skills to build/update firewall policies?
  - Process: Is the containment process effective? Is allowing the attack to continue to identify the threat entity/location a good idea (to support law enforcement)?
  - Technology: Can software tools quarantine and stop a malware attack? Is shutting down all external connections a good immediate solution (at the firewall)?

- Recovery Actions

  - People: Can the IT staff recover backup data files and media?
  - Process: What is the order of recovery? Bring up internal databases and communications first and external servers (email and web site) be reestablished later? What are the recovery time standards for the company to regain business operations? What is acceptable? What is not acceptable?
  - Technology: Are there adequate numbers of back up devices for critical systems? Can third-party service providers assist in recovering lost or damaged data?

- User Response Activities

  - People: Can employees safely return to an operational state?
  - Process: Does the company need to control access to services to select individuals first (e.g., finance, logistics, etc.)
  - Technology: Can technology resolve immediate problems from the recovery vice the employee such as, for example, reselecting printers and other data connections?

MORE COMPLETE ANSWER: In those situations when a control is specifically discussing a policy solution, the employment of automated tools, alerts, etc., should always be considered. Even the use of basic tracking tools such as Microsoft ® Excel ® and Access ® will at least demonstrate a level of positive control over the IT environment.

3.6.2 Track, document, and report incidents to appropriate officials and/or authorities both internal and external to the organization.

MINIMUM ANSWER: This control discusses the reporting requirements based on the severity of the incident as described above and within DOD's Precedence Categorization above. Ensure some form of repository is maintained that an auditor could review at any time. Another reminder is that such information should be secured and encrypted at least at the CUI/CDI level.

MORE COMPLETE ANSWER: A more complete response may include a dedicated computer server repository that could be physically disconnected from the system when not needed. This could prevent unauthorized access if an intruder is attempting to conduct intelligence collection or **reconnaissance** of the system; this would deny intruders critical network information and add confusion for their penetration activities.

Derived Security Requirements:

3.6.3 Test the organizational incident response capability.

MINIMUM ANSWER: *Test the IR Plan at least annually.* This should include both internal and external notional penetration exercises. These may include compromised logon information and passwords provided to designated IT personnel. Ensure the results of the test are documented, reviewed, and signed by senior management. An IR test event should be maintained for any future audit.

MORE COMPLETE ANSWER: *This is not a requirement of this control and poses many risks to the IT environment. Do not recommend this solution*; this would only be required based upon the sensitivity of data and Penetration Testing (PENTEST) is directed by the DOD. It is only offered for more of an appreciation of the complexity that a PENTEST entails.

A more expensive solution is hiring an outside Penetration Testing (PENTEST) company. Ensure that Rules of Engagement (ROE) are well established. Rules that should be affirmed by both the company and the PENTESTER, for example, is that no inadvertent change or destruction of data is authorized. The PENTEST company may also require a liability release for any unintentional damage caused by the PENTEST. Always coordinate with legal professionals experienced in such matters to avoid any damage or confusion created by unclear expectations of a PENTEST.

MAINTENANCE (MA)
How do you take care of IT?

The MA security is relatively easy to address with regards to the requirements of NIST 800-171. This control requires processes and procedures that provide oversight of third-party vendors that offer IT maintenance and support. While this may appear vaguely paranoid, the company is required to exercise control of all maintenance personnel that potentially will have access to the company's and DOD's resident CUI/CDI and data. This will also typically require company escorts who have been properly background checked and authorized to oversee outside workers.

Lack of maintenance or a failure to perform maintenance can result in the unauthorized disclosure of CUI/CDI. The full implementation of this requirement is contingent on the finalization of the proposed CUI/CDI federal regulation and marking guidance in the **CUI Registry**. (The marking requirements have been completed, and it is best to refer to the Registry, https://www.archives.gov/cui/registry/category-list, for specified industry codes.) These markings should be applied to business CUI/CDI data as well as IT hardware such as servers, desktops, laptops, etc.

Basic Security Requirements:

3.7.1 Perform maintenance on organizational information systems.

MINIMUM ANSWER: This should describe the company's maintenance procedures for its IT infrastructure. This could include either internal maintenance teams or third-party companies. This will include hardware component repairs and replacements, printer repairs, etc. Any maintenance agreements should be provided as artifacts to support an authorization package.

MORE COMPLETE ANSWER: Maintenance could include the identification of computer hardware spares on-site or at company warehouse locations. Operational spares should be managed by the company's logistics' personnel; they should be captured within the property book database and its associated hard copy reporting to senior management.

3.7.2 Provide effective controls on the tools, techniques, mechanisms, and personnel used to conduct information system maintenance.

MINIMUM ANSWER: This control relates to tools used for diagnostics and repairs of the company's IT system/network. These tools include, for example, hardware/software diagnostic test equipment and hardware/software **packet sniffers**. Access to the hardware tools should be secured in lockable containers, and only accessed by authorized IT personnel.

In the case of software tools, they should be restricted to personnel with privileged user rights and specifically audited when any use is required or needed.

MORE COMPLETE ANSWER: Suggested additional control may include two-person integrity requirements. This would require that when any of these types of tools are utilized, there should be at least two authorized individuals involved in any system maintenance or diagnostic activities.

Derived Security Requirements:

3.7.3 Ensure equipment removed for off-site maintenance is sanitized of any CUI.

MINIMUM ANSWER: Company data should be backed-up locally and secured for a future reinstall on another storage device or on the returned/repaired IT component. Also, the data should specifically be "wiped" by an industry-standard application for data deletion. There are many software tools that conduct multiple "passes" of data wipes to ensure sanitization of the media.

MORE COMPLETE ANSWER: Any reports produced by the data "wiping" program could be captured in an equipment data log to provide proof of the action. Maintaining a hard copy of soft copy spreadsheet or database log would be helpful. Future inspections by DOD may check this procedure to confirm the continuous application and repeatability of this procedure.

3.7.4 Check media containing diagnostic and test programs for malicious code before the media are used in the information system.

MINIMUM ANSWER: The normal solution for this is to conduct a scan using corporate anti-virus software applications.

MORE COMPLETE ANSWER: A more thorough solution would include the use of an anti-malware application. Anti-malware programs are more comprehensive and proactively monitor **endpoints**, i.e., computers, laptops, servers, etc. (Anti-virus is not always designed to identify and clean malware, adware, worms, etc., from infected storage devices).

3.7.5 Require multifactor authentication to establish nonlocal maintenance sessions via external network connections and terminate such connections when nonlocal maintenance is complete.

MINIMUM ANSWER: Nonlocal maintenance are those diagnostic or repair activities conducted over network communications to include the Internet or dedicated least circuits.

This requires that any external third-party maintenance activities use some form of Multi-Factor Authentication (MFA) to directly access company IT hardware and software components. If IT personnel, working with outside maintainers can use a MFA solution then the company most likely has a robust IT support capability. If not, then this control is a good candidate for an early POAM; ensure good milestones are established for monthly review, for example, "on-going research," "market survey of potential candidate solutions," "identification of funding sources," etc.

MORE COMPLETE ANSWER: A more complete answer requires a technical solution. As discussed earlier, the use of CAC, PIV cards, or tokens, such as the RSA ® rotating encryption keying devices are ideal solutions. This solution most likely will require additional analysis and funding approaches to select the most appropriate answer.

RSA Token (R)

3.7.6 Supervise the maintenance activities of maintenance personnel without required access authorization.

MINIMUM ANSWER: The procedure requirement should reflect that non-company maintenance personnel should always be escorted. An access log should be maintained, and it should include, for example, the individual or individuals, the represented company, the equipment repaired/diagnosed, the arrival and departure times, and the assigned escort. Maintain these hard-copy of soft-copy logs for future auditing purposes.

MORE COMPLETE ANSWER: Procedural enhancements could include confirmed background checks of third-party maintainers and picture identification compared with the on-site individual. These additional enhancements should be based upon the sensitivity of the company's data. Any unattended CUI/CDI data should always be secured in accordance with CUI/CDI procedures—in a lockable container.

MEDIA PROTECTION (MP)
Create, protect, and destroy

The MP control was written to handle the challenges of managing and protecting the computer media storing CUI/CDI. This would include DOD concerns about removable hard drives and especially the ability for a threat employ the use of a Universal Serial Bus (USB) "thumb drive."

Special Topic: DOD USB Policy
A UNIVERSAL SERIAL BUS (USB) OR **THUMB DRIVE** WHILE PROVIDING GREAT FLEXIBILITY TO MOVE DATA TO AND FROM SYSTEM DATA STORES, THEY ARE ALSO MAJOR MEANS TO INJECT MALICIOUS SOFTWARE SUCH AS VIRUSES AND RANSOMWARE INTO A COMPANY'S SECURITY BOUNDARY. DOD PROHIBITS USB USE IN DOD ENVIRONMENTS. IT'S CRITICAL TO ADDRESS THE PROPER CARE AND USE OF THESE IN A COMPANY'S IT INFRASTRUCTURE AND ASSOCIATED PROCEDURE GUIDE.

While most computer users are aware of the convenience of the thumb drive to help store, transfer, and maintain data, it is also a well-known threat vector where criminals and foreign threats can introduce serious malware and viruses into unsuspecting users' computers. DOD forbids their use except under very specific and controlled instances.

MP is also about assurances by the business that proper destruction and sanitization of old storage devices has occurred. There are many instances where DOD and other federal agencies have not implemented an effective sanitization process and inadvertent disclosure of national security data has been released into the public. Cases include salvage companies discovering hard drives and disposed computers containing CUI/CDI and, in several cases, national security classified information, has occurred.

Be especially mindful that the sanitization process requires high-grade industry or government-approved applications that completely and effectively destroys all data on the target drive. Other processes may include physical shredding of the drive or destruction methods that further prevent the reconstruction of any virtual data by unauthorized personnel.

Basic Security Requirements:

3.8.1 Protect (i.e., physically control and securely store) information system media containing CUI, both paper and digital.

MINIMUM ANSWER: To implement this control the business should establish procedures regarding both CUI/CDI physical and virtual (disk drives) media. This should include only authorized personnel having access to individual and corporate sensitive data with requisite background checks and training. A business can use the foundations of other control families to further **mitigate** or reduce risks/threats.

RISK MANAGEMENT'S FOUNDATION:

MITIGATE OR REDUCE,

NOT ELIMINATION

OF THE RISK OR THREAT

A company can use other controls such as *more* training, longer audit log retention, *more* guards, or *more* complex passwords to **mitigate** any control. This would more clearly demonstrate to DOD that the firm has a positive implementation of these security controls.

The use of other mitigating controls within NIST 800-171 are specifically about **risk reduction.** Any effort to use other families of controls to meet a specific control improves the overall IT infrastructure's security posture and is highly recommended.

MORE COMPLETE ANSWER: The MP control can be further demonstrated by safeguarding physical files in secure or fire-resistant vaults. This could also include requirements for only IT personnel issuing property hand receipts for computer equipment or devices; a good accountability system is important.

3.8.2 Limit access to CUI on information system media to authorized users.

MINIMUM ANSWER: Identify in policy documents who, by name, title or function, has access to specified CUI/CDI. Any artifacts should include the policy document and an associated by-name roster of personnel assigned access by-system, e.g., accounting system, ordering system, patent repository, medical records, etc.

MORE COMPLETE ANSWER: A more complete response could include logging of authorized personnel and providing a print-out of accesses over a one-month period.

3.8.3 Sanitize or destroy information system media containing CUI before disposal or release for reuse.

MINIMUM ANSWER: A good policy description is a must regarding data destruction of sensitive information within DOD. Either use a commercial-grade "wiping" program, or physically destroy the drive.

If the company is either planning to internally reuse or sell to outside repurposing companies, ensure that the wiping is commercial grade or approved by DOD. There are companies providing disk shredding or destruction services. Provide any service agreements that should specify the type and level of data destruction to DOD assessors.

NIST Special Publication 800-161

Supply Chain Risk Management
Practices for Federal Information
Systems and Organizations

MORE COMPLETE ANSWER: For any DOD assessment, the media sanitization company should provide **destruction certificates**. Chose several selected destruction certificates to include in the DOD BOE submission. Typically, logistics and supply ordering sections of the business should manage as part of the Supply Chain Risk Management (SCRM) process.

Supply Chain Risk Management is a relatively new concern within the federal government, but it is a major concern for DOD. It is part of securing IT products within the business.

Questions that should be considered include:

- Is this product produced by the US or by an Ally?
- Could counterfeit IT items be purchased from less-than reputable entities?
- Is this IT product from the DOD's approved hardware/software products listings?

For further information see NIST 800-161, *Supply Chain Risk Management Practices for Federal Information Systems and Organizations*.
(http://nvlpubs.nist.gov/nistpubs/SpecialPublications/NIST.SP.800-161.pdf).

Derived Security Requirements:

3.8.4 Mark media with necessary CUI markings and distribution limitations.

MINIMUM ANSWER: This includes the marking of both physical documents as well as soft-copy versions. The best way to answer this is by referencing the following National Archives and Record Administration (NARA) document as part of the company's procedural guide that addresses this control:

- *Marking Controlled Unclassified Information*, Version 1.1 – December 6, 2016. (https://www.archives.gov/files/cui/20161206-cui-marking-handbook-v1-1.pdf)

EXAMPLE PROCEDURE: All company personnel will mark CUI/CDI, physical and virtual data, in accordance with the National Archives and Record Administration (NARA), <u>Marking Controlled Unclassified Information, Version 1.1 – December 6, 2016</u>. If there are questions about marking requirements, employees will refer these questions to their immediate supervisor or the corporate CUI/CDI officer."

MORE COMPLETE ANSWER: This could include a screen capture that shows a DOD representative that onscreen access to CUI/CDI data is properly marked. A firm could also assign a CUI/CDI marking specialist; this person should be an individual with prior security experience and familiar with DOD marking requirements. For example, this individual could additionally provide quarterly "brown bag" sessions where the "CUI/CDI Security Officer" provides training during lunchtime sessions. Be creative when considering more thorough means to reinforce cybersecurity control requirements.

3.8.5 Control access to media containing CUI and maintain accountability for media during transport outside of controlled areas.

MINIMUM ANSWER: This control is about "transport outside of controlled areas." This too is a matter of only authorized individuals (couriers) be authorized by position, training, and security checks that should be considered when the company needs to transport CUI/CDI external to its typical corporate location.

Individuals should be provided either **courier cards** or **orders** that are signed by an authorized company representative typically responsible for oversight of security matters. This could be, for example, the corporate security officer, Information System Security Manager (ISSM), or their designated representative. These individuals should be readily known by other employees and managers who have demands to move CUI/CDI to outside locations. This would demonstrate there are available and on-call personnel based upon the business mission and priorities. This also should be a limited cadre of personnel that management relies on for such external courier services.

MORE COMPLETE ANSWER: The company could hire an outside contract service that transports both physical and computer media containing CUI/CDI based upon the company's mission.

3.8.6 Implement cryptographic mechanisms to protect the confidentiality of CUI stored on digital media during transport unless otherwise protected by alternative physical safeguards.

MINIMUM ANSWER: *This is a Data at Rest (DAR) issue.* See Control 3.1.3 for depiction. The recommendation is that all CUI/CDI needs to be encrypted. A common application that has been used by DOD is Bitlocker ®. It provides password protection to "lock down" any transportable media. It is not the only solution, and there are many solutions that can be used to secure DAR.

The 256-bit key length is the common standard for commercial and DOD encryption applications for hard drives, removeable drives, and even USB devices. DOD requires DAR must *always* be encrypted; it is best to resource and research acceptable tools that DOD supports and recognizes.

MORE COMPLETE ANSWER: The reinforcing of this control may include using enhanced physical security measures. This could include hardened and lockable carry cases. Only authorized employees should transport designated CUI/CDI. This should also be captured in the submitted BOE to DOD.

3.8.7 Control the use of removable media on information system components.

MINIMUM ANSWER: Identify in corporate policy the types and kinds of removeable media that can be attached to fixed desktop and laptop computers. These could include external hard drives, optical drives, or USB thumb drives.

Strongly recommend that thumb drives are not used; if needed, then designate IT security personnel who can authorize their restricted use. This should also include anti-virus/malware scans before their use.

MORE COMPLETE ANSWER: Removeable media drives can be "blocked" by changes in system **registry** settings; company IT personnel should be able to prevent such designated devices from accessing the computer and accessing the company network.

3.8.8 Prohibit the use of portable storage devices when such devices have no identifiable owner.

MINIMUM ANSWER: This should be established in the company procedure. If such devices are found, they should be surrendered to security, and scanned immediately for any viruses, malware, etc.

MORE COMPLETE ANSWER: As described in Control 3.8.7, IT personnel can block unauthorized devices from attaching to the computer/network by updating registry settings.

3.8.9 Protect the confidentiality of backup CUI at storage locations.

MINIMUM ANSWER: *This is a Data at Rest (DAR) issue.* See Control 3.1.3 for a depiction. See Control 3.8.6 for suggested requirements for the protection of CUI/CDI under a DAR solution.

MORE COMPLETE ANSWER: See Control 3.8.6 for additional means to protect CUI/CDI.

PERSONNEL SECURITY (PS)
Background Checks

This is a relatively simple control. It most likely is already implemented within the company and only requires procedural documents are provided in the submission to DOD. This should include both civil and criminal background checks using a reputable company that can process the individual background checks through the Federal Bureau of Investigation (FBI). Background Checking companies can also do other forms of personnel checks to include individual social media presence or financial solvency matters that may avoid any future embarrassment for the company.

While these checks are not well defined for company's under NIST 800-171, it should meet minimum government standards for a **Public Trust** review. Discuss with the Contract Officer what the requirements they suggest be met to provide the level of background check required to meet the NIST 800-171 requirement. Also, it is always best to work with HR and legal experts when formulating a personnel security policy to include the types and kinds of investigations are in accordance with applicable state and federal law in this area.

Basic Security Requirements:

3.9.1 Screen individuals prior to authorizing access to information systems containing CUI.

MINIMUM ANSWER: This control requires some form of background check be conducted for employees. There are number of firms that can provide criminal and civil background checks based upon individual's personal information and their fingerprints.

The company should capture its HR process regarding background checks in the company cybersecurity procedure document. It's also important to address when a reinvestigation is required. The suggestion is at least every 3 years or upon recognition by managers of potential legal occurrences that may include financial problems, domestic violence, etc. This control should be highly integrated with the company HR and legal policies.

MORE COMPLETE ANSWER: Some background companies can, for an additional fee, conduct active monitoring of individuals when major personal or financial changes occur in a person's life. Update company procedural guides with all details of the company's established process.

3.9.2 Ensure that CUI and information systems containing CUI are protected during and after personnel actions such as terminations and transfers.

MINIMUM ANSWER: This control is about procedures regarding whether termination is amicable or not. Always have clear terms about non-removal of corporate data and CUI/CDI after departure from the company to include databases, customer listings, and proprietary data/IP. This should include legal implications for violation of the policy.

MORE COMPLETE ANSWER: The technical solution could include monitoring by IT staff of all account activity during the out-processing period. This could also include immediate account lock-outs on the departure date. Also recommend that there are changes to all vault combinations, building accesses, etc., that the individual had specific access to during their tenure.

Derived Security Requirements: None.

PHYSICAL PROTECTION (PP)
Guards and moats….

Physical security is part of a company's overall protection of its people and facilities. A little-known fact is that the guiding principle for any *true* cybersecurity professional is to protect the life and safety of the people supported. This control is also about the protection of damage to corporate assets, facilities, or equipment; this includes any loss or destruction of the material computer equipment secured by the PP security control. This controls addresses the physical security that also includes such elements as guards, alarm systems, cameras, etc., that help the company protect its sensitive company data and, of course, its NIST 800-171 CUI.

There are no limits on how to harden a company's "castle walls," but for any owner, cost is always a major consideration. Protecting vital CUI/CDI while seemingly expansive under this control allows for reasonable flexibility. Again, the company should reasonably define its own success under the NIST 800-171 controls. "Success" can be defined from the company's point of view in terms of complexity or cost but must be prepared to defend any proposed solution to DOD assessors.

Basic Security Requirements:

3.10.1 Limit physical access to organizational information systems, equipment, and the respective operating environments to authorized individuals.

MINIMUM ANSWER: Of importance for this control, is limiting access to corporate data servers, backup devices, and specifically, the "computer farm." If the company is maintaining devices on its premises, then policy should address who has authorized access to such sensitive areas.

If the corporation is using an off-site **Cloud Service Provider (CSP)**, capture in part or in full sections of any CSP service agreements specific to physical security measures. Both types of computer architectures should address for example areas of interest such as access logs, after-hours access, camera monitoring, unauthorized access reporting criteria, types and kinds of network defense devices such as Intrusion Detection and Prevention Systems (IDS/IPS), etc., as part of the corporate procedure.

MORE COMPLETE ANSWER: This could include active alerting to both management and security personnel that includes phone calls, email alerts, or SMS text messages to designated company security personnel. Security measures and **alert thresholds** should be driven by the sensitivity of the data stored. Management should make **risk-based** determinations of the cost and returns on effectiveness to drive the corporate policy for this control as well as other solutions.

3.10.2 Protect and monitor the physical facility and support infrastructure for those information systems.

MINIMUM/MORE COMPLETE ANSWER: This control can be addressed in many ways by physical security measures. This should include locked doors, cipher locks, safes, security cameras, guard forces, etc. This control should be answered by the current physical protections that prevent direct entry into the company and physical access to its IT devices and networks.

 Derived Security Requirements:

3.10.3 Escort visitors and monitor visitor activity.

MINIMUM ANSWER: Much as described under the MA control above, like security measures as described in Control 3.7.6 should be employed.

MORE COMPLETE ANSWER: Also, refer to Control 3.7.6 on greater security measures that can be used to demonstrate more complete compliance with this control.

3.10.4 Maintain audit logs of physical access.

MINIMUM/MORE COMPLETE ANSWER: Refer to Control 3.7.6 for suggested audit log items. This should address personnel during operating and after hour entry into the company and its IT facilities. This should include logs specific to outside third-party vendors and subcontractors; any such procedures should also apply to those individuals who are not direct employees.

3.10.5 Control and manage physical access devices.

MINIMUM ANSWER: This control requires that physical access devices such as security badges, combinations, and physical keys are managed through both procedure and logs (physical or automated). The company needs to demonstrate to the government its positive security measures to protect its CUI/CDI data. While this control may appear easier than the technical policy control settings used by the company for its IT systems, it is no less important.

MORE COMPLETE ANSWER: If not already in place, identify and separate the physical security functions (e.g., facility security officer, etc.) from the technical security functions managed by corporate IT personnel with the requisite skills and experiences. Companies should avoid duty-creep on its cybersecurity personnel and define roles and responsibilities between its classic security functions (e.g., physical, personnel security, etc.) and the roles and responsibilities of its cyber workforce that may reduce their effectiveness of both security areas.

Cybersecurity workforce duty-creep is a real-world occurrence; Companies are unwittingly shifting overall "security" functions from classic security personnel to cybersecurity professionals creating overall security gaps for a company or agency

3.10.6 Enforce safeguarding measures for CUI at alternate work sites (e.g., telework sites).

MINIMUM ANSWER: (See Control 3.1.3 for explanation of DAR and DIT). This control can be easily addressed by DAR application solutions. Laptops should always be password protected; this should be part of any central cybersecurity policy document and enforced by technical solutions deployed by company IT personnel. Additionally, The DIT protections are afforded by corporate VPN and 2FA/MFA solutions.

MORE COMPLETE ANSWER: The company should establish minimum requirements for telework protection. This could include, for example, work should be conducted in a physically securable area, the VPN should always be used, corporate assets should not use unsecure networks such as at coffee shops, fast-food restaurants, etc. This could also include an explicit telework agreement for employees prior to being authorized telework permission, and it should be closely coordinated with HR and legal experts.

RISK ASSESSMENT (RA)
Dealing with Changes to the Infrastructure

The RA control relies on a continual process to determine whether changes in hardware, software, or architecture create either a major positive or negative **security-relevant** effect. This is typically done by using a **Change Request** (CR). If an upgrade to, for example, the Window 10 ® Secure Host Baseline Operating System software, and it improves the security posture of the network, a Risk Assessment (RA) is needed and an associated **risk analysis** should be performed by authorized technical personnel. This could take the form of a technical report that management accepts from its IT staff for approval or disapproval of the change. Management, working with its IT staff, should determine thresholds when a formal RA activity needs to occur.

The RA process affords a great amount of flexibility during the life of the system, and should be used when other-than, for example, new application or **security patches** are applied. Security patches updates are typically integrated into Operating Systems and applications. IT personnel should also regularly manually check for normal functional patches and security patch updates from the software companies' websites.

"Negative" security-relevant effects on the corporate IT infrastructure include, for example, a major re-architecture event or a move to a Cloud Service Provider. While these events may not seem "negative," NIST and DOD standards require a full reassessment. In other words, plan accordingly if the company is going to embark on a major overhaul of its IT system. There will be a need under these circumstances to consider the impacts to the company's current Authority to Operate (ATO). These types of event typically necessitate that the NIST 800-171 process be redone; prior work in terms of policies and procedures can be reused to receive an updated ATO.

The decision-tree below is designed to help a company determine when to consider an RA:

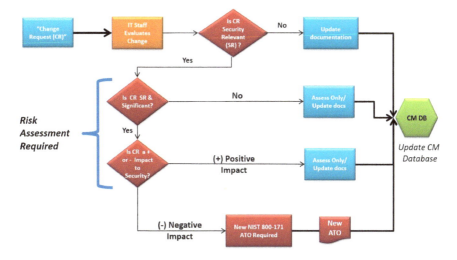

© S.R. White - Decision-tree Addressing "Security Relevance"

Basic Security Requirements:

3.11.1 Periodically assess the risk to organizational operations (including mission, functions, image, or reputation), organizational assets, and individuals, resulting from the operation of organizational information systems and the associated processing, storage, or transmission of CUI.

MINIMUM ANSWER: RA's are required when there is a "major" change due to either a hardware change (e.g., replacing an old firewall with a new Cisco ® firewall), software version upgrades (e.g., moving from Adobe ® 8.0 to 9.0), or changes to architecture (e.g., adding a new backup drive). The consideration is always about *how* this change to the baseline configuration is either a positive (normal) or negative (preferably, highly unlikely)?

It is important to describe the corporate RA process in terms of change needed and overall risk to the IT system. This should include who conducts the technical portion of the RA and who, in senior management, for example, the Chief Operating Officer (COO) or Chief Information Officer (CIO) that determines final approval.

This is as new to DOD Contracting as it is to the company; understand there will be "growing pains" as DOD continues to define its procedures

While not thoroughly discussed as part of this book, **the integration of the NIST 800-171 with DOD contracting is in its infancy**. It is best to coordinate and advise DOD Contract Officers of the changes. It is always "best practice" to maintain a history of RA development and approval for future DOD auditing.

MORE COMPLETE ANSWER: Implementing a more defined RA process could include standardized formats for RA artifacts. This could include a technical report written by knowledgeable IT personnel about a change, or a simplified form that allows for a checklist-like approach. It could also employ an outside third-party company that would formalize a review of the changes and their analysis of the overall impact to system security.

Derived Security Requirements:

3.11.2 Scan for vulnerabilities in the information system and applications periodically and when new vulnerabilities affecting the system are identified.

MINIMUM ANSWER: This control requires that the company (system owner) regularly scans for vulnerabilities in the information system and hosted applications based upon a defined frequency or randomly based upon an established policy or procedure. This is also supposed to be applied when new vulnerabilities affecting the system or applications are identified.

The simplest way to address this control is using **anti-virus** and **anti-malware** enterprise-levels of software versions. Major players in these areas include Symantec ®, McAfee ®, and

> **Reminder**
>
> **Supply Chain Risk Management (SCRM)**
>
> The Russian-based software developer, Kaspersky Lab's ® Anti-virus solutions are currently prohibited by the DOD.

Malwarebytes ®. Procedural documents should describe the products used to address "new vulnerabilities" using these solutions. See also SYSTEM AND INFORMATION INTEGRITY (SI) as a reinforcing control for this RA control.

MORE COMPLETE ANSWER: A suggested more complete implementation could be the leveraging of company ISP services also is identified for providing a secondary layer of defense as a form of "trusted" connection. This could include any available SLA's that define the service provider's ability to mitigate such additional threats by employing **whitelisting** and **blacklisting** services; these services are designed to allow or restrict access depending on an **Access Control List** (ACL). See Control 3.14.2 for a more detailed description.

3.11.3 Remediate vulnerabilities in accordance with assessments of risk.

MINIMUM ANSWER: Typically, anti-virus and anti-malware security applications cannot only detect but remove and quarantine malicious software. Update documentation accordingly.

This control also addresses "vulnerabilities" that are created by not meeting a specific control within the identified NIST 800-171 families. To address these re-assessment activities, it is normal to update system POAM documentation with explicit reasons any control is not met in full. This should attempt to answer what mitigation solutions are employed? When, by a specific date, the vulnerability will be corrected?

MORE COMPLETE ANSWER: Some additional means to better address this RA control is through other external services that can support ongoing remediation efforts. This could include the company's ISP or Cloud Service Providers. This could also include regular reviews of POAMs by both management and IT support staff personnel, for example, monthly or quarterly.

SECURITY ASSESSMENT (SA)
Beginning Continuous Monitoring and Control Reviews

The SA control is about a process that re-assesses the state of all security controls and whether changes have occurred requiring additional mitigations of new risks or threats. Within DOD, the standard is 1/3rd of the controls are to be re-assessed annually. This would require designated IT personnel conduct an SA event of approximately 36-37 controls per year. This should be captured in what is called a **ConMon Plan**. (See Appendix C, ***CONTINUOUS MONITORING: A More Detailed Discussion*** is an in-depth discussion of the current and future state of Continuous Monitoring and what it may mean to businesses).

Continuous Monitoring is a key component of the NIST 800 series cybersecurity protection framework. It is defined as "...maintaining ongoing awareness of information security, vulnerabilities, and threats to support organizational risk management decisions," (NIST Special Publication 800-137, *Information Security Continuous Monitoring (ISCM) for Federal Information Systems and Organizations*, http://nvlpubs.nist.gov/nistpubs/Legacy/SP/nistspecialpublication800-137.pdf).

ConMon is a significant guiding principle for the recurring execution of a Security Assessment

---

Basic Security Requirements:

3.12.1 Periodically assess the security controls in organizational information systems to determine if the controls are effective in their application.

MINIMUM ANSWER: As described in the opening paragraph, meeting the basic requirements of the Security Assessment control should include the creation of a ConMon Plan and a review of 33% of the controls at least annually.

MORE COMPLETE ANSWER: A more thorough execution could include more than 33% of the controls being reviewed and reassessed; it is suggested to provide the results of annual Security Assessments to DOD contracting or their designated recipients.

3.12.2 Develop and implement plans of action designed to correct deficiencies and reduce or eliminate vulnerabilities in organizational information systems.

MINIMUM ANSWER: Where the security control is not fully implemented by the company or not recognized by DOD as being fully compliant, a detailed POAM is necessary; review guidance under the AC control for a more detailed discussion of what is required in preparing a POAM for review. (See the Introduction about major requirements for completing a POAM).

As described earlier, this should include activities that are meant to answer the control in full or at least leverage other physical and virtual elements of other security controls to reinforce the posture of the control in question. A well-written POAM that is tracked and managed serves as the foundation for a strong risk management process.

> *Cybersecurity is a leadership, not a technical challenge*

MORE COMPLETE ANSWER: Regular reviews by management and IT staff should enhance the company's cybersecurity posture. Cybersecurity is not just something that IT security personnel do; it includes the active oversight and review by corporate leadership to ensure effectiveness.

3.12.3 Monitor information system security controls on an ongoing basis to ensure the continued effectiveness of the controls.

MINIMUM ANSWER: This control can be answered in terms of a well-developed and executed ConMon Plan. Describing its purpose and the actions of assigned personnel to accomplish this task will answer this control.

MORE COMPLETE ANSWER: Suggested additional efforts regarding this control could include ad hoc spot checks of controls outside of the annual review process. Identify using the **PPT Model** described in Control 3.6.1 who is responsible for conducting the assessment (people), the workflow to adequately assess the current state of the control (process), and any supporting automation that provides feedback and reporting to management (technology).

3.12.4 Develop, document, and periodically update system security plans that describe system boundaries, system environments of operation, how security requirements are implemented, and the relationships with or connections to other systems.

MINIMUM ANSWER: this control requires that the **SSP** is updated regularly. The SSP should at a minimum be reviewed *annually* by designated company cybersecurity/IT personnel to ensure its accuracy. The SSP should be specifically updated sooner if there are major changes to the:

- Hardware
- Software
- Network Architecture/Topology

MORE COMPLETE ANSWER: A more complete means to address this control is by addressing in company change control boards. These are regular meetings when changes to hardware, software or architecture occur. This should include mechanisms to document the occurrence of application and security patching. An effective procedure should always address changes to the IT system

Derived Security Requirements: None.

SYSTEM AND COMMUNICATIONS PROTECTION (SC)
External Communication and Connection Security

The overall risk management strategy is a key in establishing the appropriate technical solutions as well as procedural direction and guidance for the company. The core of this security control is it establishes policy based upon applicable federal laws, Executive Orders, directives, regulations, policies, standards, and guidance. This control focuses on information security policy that can reflect the complexity of a business and its operation with the DOD. The procedures should be established for the security of the overall IT architecture and specifically for the components (hardware and software) of the information system.

In this control, many of the prior reinforcing controls can be used in demonstrating to DOD a fuller understanding of NIST 800-171 requirements. The apparent repetition of other already developed technical solutions and procedural guides can be used as supporting these controls. However, it is important that corporate procedures are addressed individually—this is for traceability purposes of any potential current or future audit of the company's work by DOD; clear and aligned explanations of the controls will make the approval process quicker.

Basic Security Requirements:

3.13.1 Monitor, control, and protect organizational communications (i.e., information transmitted or received by organizational information systems) at the external boundaries and key internal boundaries of the information systems.

MINIMUM ANSWER: This control can be answered in the corporate procedure and include, for example, active auditing that checks for unauthorized access, individuals (external) who have had numerous failed logons, and traffic entering the network from "blacklisted" addresses, etc. The company should refer to its specific audit procedure as described in more detail under the AU control.

MORE COMPLETE ANSWER: This control could be better met as formerly discussed by using "smart" firewalls and advanced SIEM solutions. While costlier and requiring greater technical experience, corporate leadership should consider. These solutions while not necessarily cost effective for the current state of the company, it should be considered as part of any future architectural change effort. Any planning efforts should consider current and future technology purchases meant to enhance the cybersecurity posture of the company. See Appendix C for a broader description of SIEM technologies and how they may become part of the IT infrastructure.

3.13.2 Employ architectural designs, software development techniques, and systems engineering principles that promote effective information security within organizational information systems.

MINIMUM/MORE COMPLETE ANSWER: Describing effective security architectural design measures can be as simple as the employment of a properly configured firewall or 2FA/MFA utilized by the company. It is highly likely that the average company seeking contracts with DOD will be specifically concerned with basic and secure architectures.

Other **mitigation** elements that can be described for this control may include physical security measures (e.g., a 24-hour guard force, reinforced fire doors, and cameras) or blacklist measures that prevent unauthorized applications from executing in the corporate network. See Control 3.13.10 for how 2FA operates internal or external to a company's network.

Derived Security Requirements:

3.13.3 Separate user functionality from information system management functionality.

MINIMUM ANSWER: The policy should not allow privileged users to use the same credentials to access their user (e.g., email and Internet searches) and privileged user accesses. This separation of access is a basic network security principle and is intended to hamper both insider and external threats. (A suggested review of a similar control is Control 3.1.4 , and its discussion of the **segregation of duty** principle for comparison.)

MORE COMPLETE ANSWER: There are technical solutions to automate this process. The product, for example, CyberArk ® is used in many parts of the federal government to track and account for privileged user activity that is easily auditable. The ability to oversee especially privileged user activity should be readily audited and reviewed by senior company cybersecurity representatives.

3.13.4 Prevent unauthorized and unintended information transfer via shared system resources.

MINIMUM ANSWER: **Peer-to-peer** networking is not authorized within the DOD, and it is strongly suggested the corporation's network also forbids its use. This is typically part of the AUP and should be enforceable to prevent, e.g., insider threat opportunities or used by external hackers to gain unauthorized access using legitimate employee security credentials.

MORE COMPLETE ANSWER: Suggest that this is part of the normal audit activity by designated IT personnel. They could be reviewing audit logs for unauthorized connections to include peer-to-peer networking.

3.13.5 Implement subnetworks for publicly accessible system components that are physically or logically separated from internal networks.

MINIMUM/MORE COMPLETE ANSWER: The simplest answer is that subnetworks reduce an intruder's ability to effectively exploit corporate network addresses. Have IT personnel establish subnetworks specifically for the email and webservers that are in the external Demilitarized Zone (DMZ) of the corporate's security boundary; see Control 3.14.2 for the location of a DMZ relative to the company's network. Some companies maintain external database servers; ensure they too have established subnetwork addresses.

3.13.6 Deny network communications traffic by default and allow network communications traffic by exception (i.e., deny all, permit by exception).

MINIMUM/MORE COMPLETE ANSWER: Like Control 3.4.8, this control can be selected by IT personnel. This is a technical control that should also be captured in the procedure document. These network settings are typically set at the firewall and involve **whitelisting** (only permitting access by exception) and **blacklisting** (from non-authorized Internet addresses) everyone else to enter the network. (Also, review Control 3.14.2.)

3.13.7 Prevent remote devices from simultaneously establishing non-remote connections with the information system and communicating via some other connection to resources in external networks.

MINIMUM/MORE COMPLETE ANSWER: If a teleworking employee uses their remote device (i.e., notebook computer), and then connects to a non-remote (external) connection, it allows for an unauthorized external connection to exist; this provides a potential hacker with the ability to enter the network using the authorized employee's credentials.

It is critical that the company requires employees to use their VPN connection and blocks any unsecure connections from accessing internal systems or applications. IT personnel need to ensure these settings are properly configured and are part of the corporate cybersecurity procedure documentation.

3.13.8 Implement cryptographic mechanisms to prevent unauthorized disclosure of CUI during transmission unless otherwise protected by alternative physical safeguards.

MINIMUM ANSWER: Remember, this control is about external communications from the network and its system boundary. This is a DIT issue and is protected by the cryptographic solutions discussed earlier; see Control 3.1.3. Documentation should reflect the type and level of protection of data transmitted. Any additional protections such as a VPN, a **secure circuit/dedicated** circuit provided by a commercially contracted carrier may afford more security for company data transmissions.

MORE COMPLETE ANSWER: Better levels of protection could be addressed in terms of **defense in depth** which is a current operational philosophy supported by DOD; *additional layers of security provide additional defense*. (See the "Defense-in-Depth" diagram at Control 3.14.2).

3.13.9 Terminate network connections associated with communications sessions at the end of the sessions or after a defined period of inactivity.

MINIMUM ANSWER: This was addressed in the AC control specific to the complete termination of a session. Sessions of suggested importance would be those such as to the financial, HR, or other key computer server systems housing defined CUI/CDI. It is recommended that the procedure be updated specific to *this* control re-using language provided by any response to the control(s) discussing the termination of a network connection.

MORE COMPLETE ANSWER: This control can be strengthened by audit of sessions that have timed-out. SA's and IT staff can determine from audit logs that the proscribed time-out period was met and enforced. Provide a sampling to any DOD inspector as part of the final packet.

3.13.10 Establish and manage cryptographic keys for cryptography employed in the information system.

MINIMUM ANSWER: There are two major scenarios likely to occur:

1. Use of commercial cryptographic programs that resides within the company's architecture or is provided by an external "managed service" provider are the most likely scenarios. The **keys** will be maintained and secured by the cryptographic application. The company is establishing some form of 2FA solution. The **public key** would be secured somewhere else in the architecture, and the **private key**, that of the employee, would reside on a token such as CAC card or another key device.

2. Using a DOD or other like 2FA solution with a CAC, Personal Identity Verification (PIV) card or "token" such as those produced by RSA ® is likely if DOD authorizes the

exchange of keys on its systems with that of the company. This requires a **Certificate Authority (CA)** usually outside the local network either managed by DOD or another trusted commercial entity with the capability to support "asymmetric" 2FA.

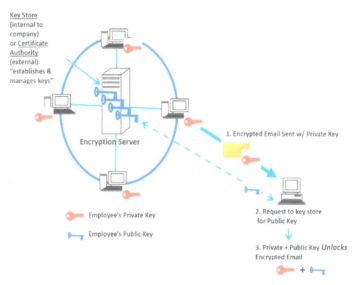

© S.R. Red - Two-factor Authentication (2FA) – Asymmetric Cryptography Basic Description

Whichever solution is used, ensure compatibility with DOD systems and other companies' as part of its normal operations. ***All transmittal of CUI/CDI data is required to be encrypted.***

MORE COMPLETE ANSWER: Any greater ability to secure and protect the **key store** within the company or through defined SLA's with outside service providers is important. Ensure they have safeguards in place to protect unauthorized access to its system as well; they may use stronger encryption methods, but ensure they are recognized by DOD and are Federal Information Processing Standards (FIPS 140-2) compliant. (See Control 3.13.11 for identifying FIPS 140-2 solutions).

3.13.11 Employ FIPS-validated cryptography when used to protect the confidentiality of CUI.

MINIMUM/MORE COMPLETE ANSWER: The company needs to confirm that its encryption applications are FIPS 140-2 compliant. It can easily be verified at the website below:

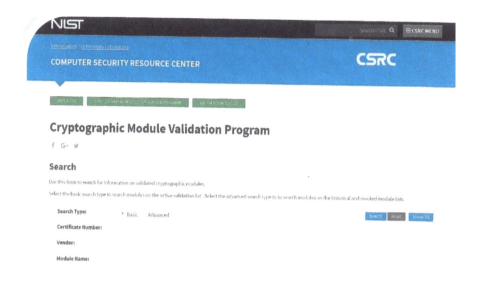

Official NIST site to confirm FIPS 140-2 cryptographic compliance
(https://csrc.nist.gov/projects/cryptographic-module-validation-program/validated-modules/search)

3.13.12 Prohibit remote activation of collaborative computing devices and provide indication of devices in use to users present at the device.

MINIMUM ANSWER: **Collaborative computing devices** include, for example, "networked white boards, cameras, and microphones." The intent is to prevent these devices being used by intruders to conduct reconnaissance of a network.

This can be prevented by changes in **registry settings** that only authorized IT personnel with privileged access can change. Furthermore, if these items are active, visible lighting or audible alerts, should be considered to notify IT and security personnel. Policy should require that individuals do not change these settings to include privileged users. Any change should only be approved by exception and require a privileged user who is authorized to make such changes.

MORE COMPLETE ANSWER: Auditing and SIEM solutions could be configured to ensure these settings are not tampered. See Control 3.3.2 for further discussion of this topic area.

3.13.13 Control and monitor the use of mobile code.

MINIMUM/MORE COMPLETE ANSWER: Mobile code is mainly part of Internet-capable business phones. The company's phone carrier can limit the types and kinds of mobile applications that reside on employee phones. Most applications are usually required to meet secure industry development standards. It is best to confirm with the company's carrier how mobile code apps are secured and restrict employees to a set number of approved mobile apps. Define in the company procedures the base applications provided to each employee, and the process for work specific applications that other specialists in the company require.

3.13.14 Control and monitor the use of Voice over Internet Protocol (VoIP) technologies.

MINIMUM ANSWER: The most likely current place VOIP would exist is the company's phone service. Ensure with the phone carrier that their VOIP services are secure and what level of security is used to protect corporate communications.   Furthermore, identify any contract information that provides details about the provided security.

MORE COMPLETE ANSWER: Verify what monitoring services and network protection (from malware, viruses, etc.) are part of the current service plan. If necessary, determine whether both the control and monitoring are included or extra services. If not fully included, consider formulating a POAM.

3.13.15 Protect the authenticity of communications sessions.

MINIMUM/ MORE COMPLETE ANSWER: This control addresses communications' protection and establishes confidence that the session is authentic; it ensures the identity of the individual and the information being transmitted. Authenticity protection includes, for example, protecting against session hijacking or insertion of false information.

This can be resolved by some form, hard or soft token MFA/2FA, solution. It will ensure the identity and FIPS 140-2 encryption to prevent data manipulation. See Control 3.5.2 for further discussion. While these are not absolute solutions, they greatly demonstrate more certainty that the communications are authentic.

3.13.16 Protect the confidentiality of CUI at rest.

MINIMUM ANSWER: This is a DAR issue, and as discussed earlier, it is a DOD requirement. Ensure the proper software package is procured that meets FIPS 140-2 standards. (See Control 3.13.11 for NIST's website information).

MORE COMPLETE ANSWER: If using a CSP, ensure it is using DOD accepted FIPS 140-2 standards; it will make authorization simpler. And, a reminder, if the business cannot use FIPS 140-2 solutions, ensures an effective POAM is developed that addresses why it cannot be currently implemented and when the company is prepared to implement the control. *When will the company be compliant?*

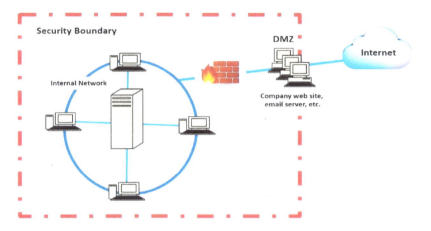

© S.R. Red - Basic Company Network View

- **Blacklisting** is used to block known "bad guys." There are companies and the DOD that can provide lists of known malicious sites based upon their Internet address. Blacklists require continuous management to be most effective.

Both solutions are not guaranteed. While they afford additional means to slow hackers and nation-state intruders, they are not total solutions. Therefore DOD, and much of the cybersecurity community, strongly supports the principle of **defense in depth** where other technological solutions help to reinforce the protections because of security programming flaws inadvertently created by software developers and the constant challenge of hackers exploiting various areas of modern IT architectures to conduct their nefarious actions.

The Principle of Defense in Depth

3.14.3 Monitor information system security alerts and advisories and take appropriate actions in response.

MINIMUM ANSWER: This SI control can be best met through auditing. This can be met by using applications (such as anti-virus) or tools embedded within the architecture. These should include Intrusion Detection capabilities, network packet capture tools such as Wireshark ®, or audit logs. The process and associated actions should include recognition and notification to senior management. Management should ensure developed processes define when an event is raised to a level of a notifiable **incident** to DOD.

MORE COMPLETE ANSWER: A more complete solution could use other advanced tool sets based upon the education and experience of the IT support staff. These could include malicious code protection software (such as found in more advance anti-malware solutions). Consideration should always include the overall ROI for the investment in such tools.

If the company can only implement minor portions of the control and has the planned intent to invest in improved tools in the future, it is best to develop a well-defined POAM with achievable milestones for the company to pursue. It will demonstrate to DOD a commitment to improving cybersecurity vice ignoring other technical methods to reduce the risk to the company and its associated CUI/CDI.

Derived Security Requirements:

3.14.4 Update malicious code protection mechanisms when new releases are available.

MINIMUM/COMPLETE ANSWER: This is usually easily resolved through ongoing software license agreements with vendors for malicious code internal programs or external contracted support services. Assuming a new version is made available during the active period of the license, updates are typically free; document the company's procedure for maintaining not only current, but legal versions of malicious code detection and prevention software or services.

3.14.5 Perform periodic scans of the information system and real-time scans of files from external sources as files are downloaded, opened, or executed.

MINIMUM ANSWER: Many of the solutions already discussed afford real-time scanning of files and traffic as they traverse the network. Scanning of files should always be conducted from external downloads for both viruses and malware. Ensure the technical policy settings are always set to conduct real-time scans of the network, endpoints (i.e., work computers both internal and used by teleworking employees), and files entering the network by the appropriate tools to ensure network operation and security.

MORE COMPLETE ANSWER: Require IT personnel to regularly check that real-time scanning has not been changed accidently or on purpose. It is important to be aware that potential intruders will attempt to shut down any security features such as active scanning. Train IT personnel to manually check at least weekly and alert management if the changes are suspicious. identifying possible entry into the company's data is a function of the SI as well as a major component of the AU control family.

3.14.6 Monitor the information system including inbound and outbound communications traffic, to detect attacks and indicators of potential attacks.

MINIMUM ANSWER: As discussed, anti-virus and malware provide some level of checking of inbound and outbound traffic. Document both manual and automated means to ensure traffic is monitored.

Procedures should identify the **people** who will conduct regular review, the **process** that ensures proper oversight is in place to identify violations of this control, and what **technologies** are being used to protect inbound and outbound traffic from attack. (See Control 3.6.1 for discussion about the **PPT Model**, and its application to address security controls).

MORE COMPLETE ANSWER: This could also identify commercial ISP's supporting the business with a "trusted" connections to the Internet. Refer to provided SLA's and provided contract information for DOD review.

3.14.7 Identify unauthorized use of the information system.

MINIMUM ANSWER: This is met through active and regular auditing of, for example, systems, applications, intrusion detections, and firewall logs. It is important to recognize that there may be limitations for the IT staff to properly and adequately review all available logs created by the company's IT network. It is best to identify the critical logs to review regularly and any secondary logs as time permits. Avoid trying to review all available system logs; there are many. Also, determine the level of effort, required processing time, ability, and training of the company's' IT support staff.

MORE COMPLETE ANSWER: In addition to the above, consider third-party companies that can provide a monitoring service of the network. While these may be expensive, it will depend on the business, its mission, and the critically of the data. This solution will require a well-developed SLA's with appropriate oversight to ensure the company receives the Quality of Service (QOS) the company needs.

CONCLUSION

This is Risk Management, NOT Risk Elimination

The major premise of the NIST cybersecurity process is to recognize that it's not about the absolute certainty that the security controls will stop every type of cyber-attack. Risk Management is about recognizing the system's overall weaknesses. It's about the company's leadership, not just the IT staff, has identified where those weaknesses exist.

Risk Management is also about a defined Continuous Monitoring (ConMon) and effective Risk Assessment processes. Such processes afford the needed protections to a company's sensitive CUI/CDI. These are not meant to be complete answers to an ever-changing risk landscape. It is only through an active and continual review of the controls can DOD or companies ensure near-certainty their networks are as secure *as possible*.

The objective of this book is to provide a basic understanding of the controls, how to effectively respond to them, and meet NIST 800-171 requirements to authorize a company to conduct business within DOD. While DOD may be the first federal agency to mandate NIST 800-171 implementation, expect other agencies such as the Department of Homeland Security (DHS), the Department of Commerce (DOC), home of NIST, and Department of Energy (DOE), to be the next likely candidates to necessitate businesses to meet NIST 800-171.

A final objective of this effort was to provide a plain-English and how-to guide for the non-IT business owner. The target of this book is to provide information that they and their IT staffs can critically think about how to best respond to these 110 designated controls. This book provides a constructive starting point for small through big business to not only meet the requirements of NIST 800-171, but to truly protect its computers, systems, and data from the "bad guys" near and far.

APPENDIX A -- RELEVANT REFERENCES

Federal Information Security Modernization Act of 2014 (P.L. 113-283), December 2014.
http://www.gpo.gov/fdsys/pkg/PLAW-113publ283/pdf/PLAW-113publ283.pdf

Executive Order 13556, *Controlled Unclassified Information*, November 2010.
http://www.gpo.gov/fdsys/pkg/FR-2010-11-09/pdf/2010-28360.pdf

Executive Order 13636, *Improving Critical Infrastructure Cybersecurity*, February 2013.
http://www.gpo.gov/fdsys/pkg/FR-2013-02-19/pdf/2013-03915.pdf

National Institute of Standards and Technology Federal Information Processing Standards
Publication 200 (as amended), *Minimum Security Requirements for Federal Information
and Information Systems*.
http://csrc.nist.gov/publications/fips/fips200/FIPS-200-final-march.pdf

National Institute of Standards and Technology Special Publication 800-53 (as amended),
Security and Privacy Controls for Federal Information Systems and Organizations.
http://dx.doi.org/10.6028/NIST.SP.800-53r4

National Institute of Standards and Technology Special Publication 800-171, rev. 1,
Protecting Controlled Unclassified Information in Nonfederal Information Systems and Organizations.
https://nvlpubs.nist.gov/nistpubs/SpecialPublications/NIST.SP.800-171r1.pdf

National Institute of Standards and Technology Special Publication 800-171A, *Assessing Security
Requirements for Controlled Unclassified Information*
https://csrc.nist.gov/CSRC/media/Publications/sp/800-171a/draft/sp800-171A-draft.pdf

National Institute of Standards and Technology *Framework for Improving Critical
Infrastructure Cybersecurity* (as amended).
http://www.nist.gov/cyberframework

APPENDIX B -- RELEVANT TERMS & GLOSSARY

Audit log.	A chronological record of information system activities, including records of system accesses and operations performed in a given period.
Authentication.	Verifying the identity of a user, process, or device, often as a prerequisite to allowing access to resources in an information system.
Availability.	Ensuring timely and reliable access to and use of information.
Baseline Configuration.	A documented set of specifications for an information system, or a configuration item within a system, that has been formally reviewed and agreed on at a given point in time, and which can be changed only through change control procedures.
Blacklisting.	The process used to identify: (i) software programs that are not authorized to execute on an information system; or (ii) prohibited websites.
Confidentiality.	Preserving authorized restrictions on information access and disclosure, including means for protecting personal privacy and proprietary information.
Configuration Management.	A collection of activities focused on establishing and maintaining the integrity of information technology products and information systems, through control of processes for initializing, changing, and monitoring the configurations of those products and systems throughout the system development life cycle.
Controlled Unclassified Information (CUI/CDI).	Information that law, regulation, or governmentwide policy requires to have safeguarding or disseminating controls, excluding information that is classified under Executive Order 13526, Classified National Security Information, December 29, 2009, or any predecessor or successor order, or the Atomic Energy Act of 1954, as amended.
External network.	A network not controlled by the company.
FIPS-validated cryptography.	A cryptographic module validated by the Cryptographic Module Validation Program (CMVP) to meet requirements specified in FIPS Publication 140-2 (as amended). As a prerequisite to CMVP validation, the cryptographic module is required to employ a cryptographic algorithm implementation that has successfully passed validation testing by the Cryptographic Algorithm Validation Program (CAVP).

Hardware.	The physical components of an information system.
Incident.	An occurrence that actually or potentially jeopardizes the confidentiality, integrity, or availability of an information system or the information the system processes, stores, or transmits or that constitutes a violation or imminent threat of violation of security policies, security procedures, or acceptable use policies.
Information Security.	The protection of information and information systems from unauthorized access, use, disclosure, disruption, modification, or destruction to provide confidentiality, integrity, and availability.
Information System.	A discrete set of information resources organized for the collection, processing, maintenance, use, sharing, dissemination, or disposition of information.
Information Technology.	Any equipment or interconnected system or subsystem of equipment that is used in the automatic acquisition, storage, manipulation, management, movement, control, display, switching, interchange, transmission, or reception of data or information by the executive agency. It includes computers, ancillary equipment, software, firmware, and similar procedures, services (including support services), and related resources.
Integrity.	Guarding against improper information modification or destruction and includes ensuring information non-repudiation and authenticity.
Internal Network.	A network where: (i) the establishment, maintenance, and provisioning of security controls are under the direct control of organizational employees or contractors; or (ii) cryptographic encapsulation or similar security technology implemented between organization-controlled endpoints, provides the same effect (at least with regard to confidentiality and integrity).
Malicious Code.	Software intended to perform an unauthorized process that will have adverse impact on the confidentiality, integrity, or availability of an information system. A virus, worm, Trojan horse, or other code-based entity that infects a host. Spyware and some forms of adware are also examples of malicious code.
Media.	Physical devices or writing surfaces including, but not limited to, magnetic tapes, optical disks, magnetic disks, and printouts (but not including display media) onto which information is recorded, stored, or printed within an information system.

Mobile Code.	Software programs or parts of programs obtained from remote information systems, transmitted across a network, and executed on a local information system without explicit installation or execution by the recipient.
Mobile device.	A portable computing device that: (i) has a small form factor such that it can easily be carried by a single individual; (ii) is designed to operate without a physical connection (e.g., wirelessly transmit or receive information); (iii) possesses local, nonremovable or removable data storage; and (iv) includes a self-contained power source. Mobile devices may also include voice communication capabilities, on-board sensors that allow the devices to capture information, and/or built-in features for synchronizing local data with remote locations. Examples include smartphones, tablets, and E-readers.
Multifactor Authentication.	Authentication using two or more different factors to achieve authentication. Factors include: (i) something you know (e.g., password/PIN); (ii) something you have (e.g., cryptographic identification device, token); or (iii) something you are (e.g., biometric).
Nonfederal Information System.	An information system that does not meet the criteria for a federal information system. nonfederal organization.
Network.	Information system(s) implemented with a collection of interconnected components. Such components may include routers, hubs, cabling, telecommunications controllers, key distribution centers, and technical control devices.
Portable storage device.	An information system component that can be inserted into and removed from an information system, and that is used to store data or information (e.g., text, video, audio, and/or image data). Such components are typically implemented on magnetic, optical, or solid state devices (e.g., floppy disks, compact/digital video disks, flash/thumb drives, external hard disk drives, and flash memory cards/drives that contain nonvolatile memory).
Privileged Account.	An information system account with authorizations of a privileged user.
Privileged User.	A user that is authorized (and therefore, trusted) to perform security-relevant functions that ordinary users are not authorized to perform.
Remote Access.	Access to an organizational information system by a user (or a process acting on behalf of a user) communicating through an external network (e.g., the Internet).

Risk.	A measure of the extent to which an entity is threatened by a potential circumstance or event, and typically a function of: (i) the adverse impacts that would arise if the circumstance or event occurs; and (ii) the likelihood of occurrence. Information system-related security risks are those risks that arise from the loss of confidentiality, integrity, or availability of information or information systems and reflect the potential adverse impacts to organizational operations (including mission, functions, image, or reputation), organizational assets, individuals, other organizations, and the Nation.
Sanitization.	Actions taken to render data written on media unrecoverable by both ordinary and, for some forms of sanitization, extraordinary means. Process to remove information from media such that data recovery is not possible. It includes removing all classified labels, markings, and activity logs.
Security Control.	A safeguard or countermeasure prescribed for an information system or an organization designed to protect the confidentiality, integrity, and availability of its information and to meet a set of defined security requirements.
Security Control Assessment.	The testing or evaluation of security controls to determine the extent to which the controls are implemented correctly, operating as intended, and producing the desired outcome with respect to meeting the security requirements for an information system or organization.
Security Functions.	The hardware, software, and/or firmware of the information system responsible for enforcing the system security policy and supporting the isolation of code and data on which the protection is based.
Threat.	Any circumstance or event with the potential to adversely impact organizational operations (including mission, functions, image, or reputation), organizational assets, individuals, other organizations, or the Nation through an information system via unauthorized access, destruction, disclosure, modification of information, and/or denial of service.
Whitelisting.	The process used to identify: (i) software programs that are authorized to execute on an information system.

NOTE: CM in this article is about Continuous Monitoring (ConMon) activities discussed in greater depth; it should not be confused with discussion in this book regarding Configuration Management.

Continuous Monitoring: A More Detailed Discussion

Cybersecurity is not about shortcuts. There are no easy solutions to years of leaders demurring their responsibility to address the growing threats in cyberspace. We hoped that the Office of Personnel Management (OPM) breach several years ago would herald the needed focus, energy and funding to quash the bad-guys. That has proven an empty hope where leaders have abrogated their responsibility to lead in cyberspace. The "holy grail" solution of Continuous Monitoring (CM) has been the most misunderstood solution where too many shortcuts are perpetrated by numerous federal agencies and the private sector to create an illusion of success. This paper is specifically written to help leaders better understand what constitutes a true statement of: "we have continuous monitoring." This is not about shortcuts. This is about education, training, and understanding at the highest leadership levels that cybersecurity is not a technical issue, but a leadership issue.

The Committee on National Security Systems defines CM as: "[t]he processes implemented to maintain current security status for one or more information systems on which the operational mission of the enterprise depends," (CNSS, 2010). CM has been described as the holistic solution of end-to-end cybersecurity coverage and the answer to providing an effective global Risk Management (RM) solution. It promises the elimination of the 3-year recertification cycle that has been the bane of cybersecurity professionals.

For CM to become a reality for any agency it must meet the measures and expectations as defined in National Institute of Standards and Technology (NIST) Special Publication (SP) 800-137, *Information Security Continuous Monitoring for Federal Information Systems and Organizations.* "Continuous monitoring has evolved as a best practice for managing risk on an ongoing basis," (SANS Institute, 2016); it is an instrument that supports effective, continual, and recurring RM assurances. For any agency to truly espouse it has attained full CM compliance, it must be able to coordinate all the described major elements as found in NIST SP 800-137.

CM is not just the *passive* visibility pieces, but also includes the *active* efforts of vulnerability scanning, threat alert, reduction, mitigation, or elimination in a dynamic Information Technology (IT) environment. The Department of Homeland Security (DHS) has couched its approach to CM more holistically. Their program to protect government networks is more aptly called: "Continuous Diagnostics and Monitoring" or CDM and includes a need to react to an active network attacker. "The ability to make IT networks, end-points and applications visible; to identify malicious activity; and, to *respond* [emphasis added] immediately is critical to defending information systems and networks," (Sann, 2016).

Another description of CM can be found in NIST's *CAESARS Framework Extension: An Enterprise Continuous Monitoring Technical Reference Model (Second Draft).* It defines its essential characteristics within the concept of "Continuous Security Monitoring." It is described as a "...risk management approach to Cybersecurity that maintains a picture of an organization's security posture, provides visibility into assets, leverages use of automated data feeds, monitors effectiveness of security controls, and enables prioritization of remedies," (NIST, 2012); it must demonstrate visibility, data feeds, measures of effectiveness and allow for solutions. It provides another description of what should be demonstrated to ensure full CM designation under the NIST standard.

The government's Federal Risk and Authorization Management Program (Fed RAMP) has defined similar CM goals. These objectives are all key outcomes of a successful CM implementation. Its "... goal[s]...[are] to provide: (i) operational visibility; (ii) annual self-attestations on security control implementations; (iii) managed change control; (iv) and attendance to incident response duties," (GSA, 2012). These objectives, while not explicit to NIST SP 800-37, are well-aligned with the desires of an effective and complete solution.

RMF creates the structure and documentation needs of CM; CM represents the specific implementation and oversight of Information Security (IS) within an IT environment. It supports the general activity of RM within an agency. (See Figure 1 below). The RMF "... describes a disciplined and structured process that integrates information security and risk management activities into the system development life cycle," (NIST-B, 2011). RMF is the structure that both describes and relies upon CM as its risk oversight and effectiveness mechanism between IS and RM.

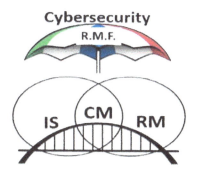

Figure 1. © S.R. Red - CM "bridges" Information Security and Risk Management

This article provides a conceptual framework to address how an agency would approach identifying a true CM solution through NIST SP 800-137. It discusses the additional need to align component requirements with the *"11 Security Automation Domains"* that are necessary to implement true CM. (See Figure 2 below). It is through the complete implementation and

Figure 2. The 11 Security Automation Domains (NIST, 2011)

integration with the other described components—See Figure 3 below--that an organization can correctly state it has achieved CM.

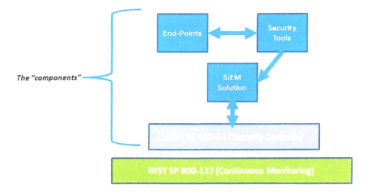

Figure 3. © S.R. Red - The "Components" of an Effective Continuous Monitoring

Continuous Monitoring – First Generation

For CM to be effective and genuine, it must align end-point visibility with security monitoring tools. This includes security monitoring tools with connectivity to "end-points" such as laptops, desktops, servers, routers, firewalls, etc. Additionally, these must work with a highly integrated Security Information and Event Management (SIEM) device. The other "component" is a clear linkage between the end-points, security monitoring tools, and the SIEM appliance, working with the *Security Automation Domains* (See Figure 2). These would include, for example, the areas of malware detection, asset and event management. CM must first address these collective components to create a "First Generation" instantiation.

More specifically, a SIEM appliance provides the central core data processing capabilities to effectively coordinate all the inputs and outputs from across the IT enterprise. It manages the data integration and interpretation of all CM components. And, it provides the necessary visibility and intelligence for an active incident response capability.

In describing a *First Generation* implemention, the following arithmetic expression is offered:

END-POINTS VISIBILITY **+ SECURITY TOOLS** MONITORING **+**
SECURITY CONTROLS ALIGNMENT **→ (INPUT) SIEM SOLUTION →**
11 SECURITY AUTOMATION DOMAINS COMPARISON **→**
(OUTPUT) [VISIBILITY + ANALYSIS + ALERTS] = CM FIRST GEN

© S.R. White – An Arithmetic Expression for First Generation Continuous Monitoring

End-point devices must be persistently visible to the applicable security devices. Together, these parts must align with the respective security controls as described in NIST SP 800-53. The selected SIEM tool must be able to accept these inputs and analyze them against defined security policy settings, recurring vulnerability scans, signature-based threats and heuristic/activity-based analyses to ensure the environment's security posture. The outputs of the SIEM must support further visibility of the IT environment, conduct and disseminate vital intelligence, and alert leadership to any ongoing or imminent dangers. The expression above is designed to provide a conceptual representation for the cybersecurity professional attempting to ascertain effective CM implementation or to develop a complete CM answer for an agency or corporation.

Additionally, the SIEM must distribute data feeds in near-real time to analysts and key leaders. It provides for multi-level "dashboard" data streams and issues alerts based upon prescribed policy settings. Once these base, *First Generation* functionalities are *consistently* aligning with the *Security Automation Domains*, then an organization or corporation can definitively express it meets the requirements of CM.

End-Points

It is necessary to identify hardware and software configuration items that must be known and constantly traceable before implementing CM within an enterprise IT environment. End-point visibility is not just the hardware devices, but the baseline software of each hardware device on the network.

Configuration Management *is* also a foundational requirement for any organization's security posture. Soundly implemented Configuration Management must be the basis of any complete CM implementation. At the beginning of any IS effort, cyber-professionals must know the current "as-is" hardware and software component state within the enterprise. End-points must be protected and monitored because they are the most valuable target for would-be hackers and cyber-thieves.

Configuration Management provides the baseline that establishes a means to identify potential compromise between the enterprise's end-points and the requisite security tools. "Organizations with a robust and effective [Configuration Management] process need to consider information security implications with respect to the development and operation of information systems including hardware, software, applications, and documentation," (NIST-A, 2011).

The RMF requires the categorization of systems and data as high, moderate, or low in terms of risk. The Federal Information Processing Standards (FIPS) Publication 199 methodology is typically used to establish data sensitivity levels in the federal government. FIPS 199 aids the cybersecurity professional in determining data protection standards of both end-points and the data stored within these respective parts. For example, a system that collects and retains sensitive data, such as financial information, requires a greater level of security. It is important that end-points are recognized as repositories of highly valued data to cyber-threats.

Further, cyber-security professionals must be constantly aware of the "…administrative and technological costs of offering a high degree of protection for all federal systems…," (Ross, Katzke, & Toth, 2005). This is just not a matter of recognizing the physical end-point alone but the value and associated costs of the virtual data stored, monitored, and protected on a continual basis. FIPS 199 assists system owners in determining whether a higher level of protection is warranted, with higher associated costs, based upon an overall FIPS 199 evaluation.

Security Tools

Security monitoring tools must identify in near-real time an active threat. Examples include anti-virus or anti-malware applications used to monitor network and end-point activities. Products like McAfee and Symantec provide enterprise capabilities that help to identify and reduce threats.

Other security tools would address in whole or part the remaining NIST *Security Automation Domains*. These would include, for example, tools to provide asset visibility, vulnerability detection, patch management updates, etc. But it is also critical to recognize that even the best current security tools are not necessarily capable to defend against all attacks. New malware or zero-day attacks pose continual challenges to the cybersecurity workforce.

For example, DHS's EINSTEIN system would not have stopped the 2015 Office of Personnel Management breach. Even DHS's latest iteration of EINSTEIN, EINSTEIN 3, an advanced network monitoring and response system designed to protect federal governments' networks, would have not stopped that attack. "...EINSTEIN 3 would not have been able to catch a threat that [had] no known footprints, according to multiple industry experts," (Sternstein, 2015).

Not until there is a much greater integration and availability of cross-cutting intelligence and more capable security tools, can any single security tool ever be fully effective. The need for multiple security monitoring tools that provide "defense in depth" may be a better protective strategy. However, with multiple tools monitoring the same *Security Automation Domains*, such an approach will certainly increase the costs of maintaining a secure agency or corporate IT environment. A determination of Return on Investment (ROI) balanced against a well-defined threat risk scoring approach is further needed at all levels of the federal and corporate IT workspace.

Security Controls

"Organizations are required to adequately mitigate the risk arising from use of information and information systems in the execution of missions and business functions," (NIST, 2013). This is accomplished by the selection and implementation of NIST SP 800-53, Revision 4, described security controls. (See Figure 4 below). They are organized into eighteen families to address sub-set security areas such as access control, physical security, incident response, etc. The use of these controls is typically tailored by the security categorization by the respective system owner relying upon FIPS 199 categorization standards. A higher security categorization requires the greater implementation of these controls.

ID	FAMILY	ID	FAMILY
AC	Access Control	MP	Media Protection
AT	Awareness and Training	PE	Physical and Environmental Protection
AU	Audit and Accountability	PL	Planning
CA	Security Assessment and Authorization	PS	Personnel Security
CM	Configuration Management	RA	Risk Assessment
CP	Contingency Planning	SA	System and Services Acquisition
IA	Identification and Authentication	SC	System and Communications Protection
IR	Incident Response	SI	System and Information Integrity
MA	Maintenance	PM	Program Management

**Note that these are all the control families required within DOD. Under the NIST 800-171 effort, not all control families are used or required.

Figure 4. Security Control Identifiers and Family Names, (NIST, 2013)

Security Information and Event Management (SIEM) Solutions

The SIEM tool plays a pivotal role in any viable "First Generation" implementation. Based upon NIST and DHS guidance, an effective SIEM appliance must provide the following functionalities:

- "Aggregate data from "across a diverse set" of security tool sources;
- Analyze the multi-source data;
- Engage in explorations of data based on changing needs
- Make quantitative use of data for security (not just reporting) purposes including the development and use of risk scores; and
- Maintain actionable awareness of the changing security situation on a real-time basis," (Levinson, 2011).

"Effectiveness is further enhanced when the output is formatted to provide information that is specific, measurable, actionable, relevant, and timely," (NIST, 2011). The SIEM device is the vital core of a full solution that collects, analyzes, and alerts the cyber-professional of potential and actual dangers in their environment.

There are several major SIEM solutions that can effectively meet the requirements of NIST SP 800-137. They include products, for example, IBM® Security, Splunk®, and Hewlett Packard's® ArcSight® products.

For example, Logrhythm ® was highly rated in the 2014 SIEM evaluation. Logrhythm® provided network event monitoring and alerts of potential security compromises. The implementation of an enterprise grade SIEM solution is necessary to meet growing cybersecurity requirements for auditing of security logs and capabilities to respond to cyber-incidents. SIEM products will continue to play a critical and evolving role in the demands for "...increased security and rapid response to events throughout the network," (McAfee® Foundstone Professional Services®, 2013). Improvements and upgrades of SIEM tools are critical to providing a more highly responsive capability for future generations of these appliances in the marketplace.

Next Generations

Future generations of CM would include specific expanded capabilities and functionalities of the SIEM device. These second generation and beyond evolutions would be more effective solutions in future dynamic and hostile network environments. Such advancements might also include increased access to a greater pool of threat database signature repositories, or more expansive heuristics that could identify active anomalies within a target network.

Another futuristic capability might include the use of Artificial Intelligence (AI). Improved capabilities of a SIEM appliance with AI augmentation would further enhance human threat analysis and provide for more automated responsiveness. "The concept of predictive analysis involves using statistical methods and decision tools that analyze current and historical data to make predictions about future events...," (SANS Institute). The next generation would boost human response times and abilities to defend against attacks in a matter of milli-seconds vice hours.

Finally, in describing the next generations of CM, it is not only imperative to expand data, informational and intelligence inputs for new and more capable SIEM products, but that input and comparative data sets must also be more fully vetted for completeness and accuracy. Increased access to signature and heuristic activity-based analysis databases would provide greater risk reduction. Greater support from private industry and the Intelligence Community would also be major improvements for Agencies that are constantly struggling against a more-capable and better resourced threat.

CM will not be a reality until vendors and agencies can integrate the right people, processes and technologies. "Security needs to be positioned as an enabler of the organization—it must take its place alongside human resources, financial resources, sound business processes and strategies, information technology, and intellectual capital as the elements of success for accomplishing the mission," (Caralli, 2004). CM is not just a technical solution. It requires capable organizations with trained personnel, creating effective policies and procedures with the requisite technologies to stay ahead of the growing threats in cyberspace.

Figure 6 below provides a graphic depiction of what CM components are needed to create a holistic NIST SP 800-137-compliant solution; this demonstrates a *First-Generation* representation. There are numerous vendors describing that they have the "holy grail" solution, but until they can prove they meet this description in total, it is unlikely they have yet a complete implementation of a thorough CM solution.

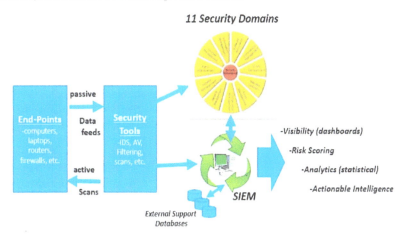

Figure 6. © S.R. Red - First Generation Continuous Monitoring

Footnotes for "Continuous Monitoring: A More Detailed Discussion"

Balakrishnan, B. (2015, October 6). *Insider Threat Mitigation Guidance* . Retrieved from SANS Institute Infosec Reading Room: https://www.sans.org/reading-room/whitepapers/monitoring/insider-threat-mitigation-guidance-36307

Caralli, R. A. (2004, December). *Managing Enterprise Security (CMU/SEI-2004-TN-046).* Retrieved from Software Engineering Institute: http://www.sei.cmu.edu/reports/04tn046.pdf

Committee on National Security Systems. (2010, April 26). *National Information Assurance (IA) Glossary.* Retrieved from National Counterintelligence & Security Center: http://www.ncsc.gov/nittf/docs/CNSSI-4009_National_Information_Assurance.pdf

Department of Defense. (2014, March 12). *DOD Instructions 8510.01: Risk Management Framework (RMF) for DoD Information Technology (IT).* Retrieved from Defense Technical Information Center (DTIC): http://www.dtic.mil/whs/directives/corres/pdf/851001_2014.pdf

GSA. (2012, January 27). *Continuous Monitoring Strategy & Guide, v1.1.* Retrieved from General Services Administration: http://www.gsa.gov/graphics/staffoffices/Continuous_Monitoring_Strategy_Guide_072712.pdf

Joint Medical Logistics Functional Development Center. (2015). JMLFDC Continuous Monitoring Strategy Plan and Procedure. Ft Detrick, MD.

Kavanagh, K. M., Nicolett, M., & Rochford, O. (2014, June 25). *Magic Quadrant for Security Information and Event Management.* Retrieved from Gartner: http://www.gartner.com/technology/reprints.do?id=1-1W8AO4W&ct=140627&st=sb&mkt_tok=3RkMMJWWfF9wsRolsqrJcO%2FhmjTEU5z17u8lWa%2B0gYkz2EFye%2BLIHETpodcMTcVkNb%2FYDBceEJhqyQJxPr3FKdANz8JpRhnqAA%3D%3D

Kolenko, M. M. (2016, February 18). *SPECIAL-The Human Element of Cybersecurity*. Retrieved from Homeland Security Today.US: http://www.hstoday.us/briefings/industry-news/single-article/special-the-human-element-of-cybersecurity/54008efd46e93863f54db0f7352dde2c.html

Levinson, B. (2011, October). *Federal Cybersecurity Best Practices Study: Information Security Continuous Monitoring.* Retrieved from Center for Regulatory Effectiveness: http://www.thecre.com/fisma/wp-content/uploads/2011/10/Federal-Cybersecurity-Best-Practice.ISCM_2.pdf

McAfee® Foundstone® Professional Services. (2013). *McAfee.* Retrieved from White Paper: Creating and Maintaining a SOC: http://www.mcafee.com/us/resources/white-papers/foundstone/wp-creating-maintaining-soc.pdf

NIST. (2011-A, August). *NIST SP 800-128: Guide for Security-Focused Configuration Management of Information Systems.* Retrieved from NIST Computer Security Resource Center: http://csrc.nist.gov/publications/nistpubs/800-128/sp800-128.pdf

NIST. (2011-B, September). *Special Publication 800-137: Information Security Continuous Monitoring (ISCM) for Federal Information Systems and Organizations.* Retrieved from NIST Computer Security Resource Center: http://csrc.nist.gov/publications/nistpubs/800-137/SP800-137-Final.pdf

NIST. (2012, January). *NIST Interagency Report 7756: CAESARS Framework Extension: An Enterprise Continuous Monitoring Technical Reference Model (Second Draft), .* Retrieved from NIST Computer Resource Security Center: http://csrc.nist.gov/publications/drafts/nistir-7756/Draft-NISTIR-7756_second-public-draft.pdf

NIST. (2013, April). *NIST SP 800-53, Rev 4: Security and Privacy Controls for Federal Information Systems .* Retrieved from NIST: http://nvlpubs.nist.gov/nistpubs/SpecialPublications/NIST.SP.800-53r4.pdf

Ross, R., Katzke, S., & Toth, P. (2005, October 17). *The New FISMA Standards and Guidelines Changing the Dynamic of Information Security for the Federal Government.* Retrieved from Information Technology Promotion Agency of Japan: https://www.ipa.go.jp/files/000015362.pdf

Sann, W. (2016, January 8). *The Key Missing Piece of Your Cyber Strategy? Visibility.* Retrieved from Nextgov: http://www.nextgov.com/technology-news/tech-insider/2016/01/key-missing-element-your-cyber-strategy-visibility/124974/

SANS Institute. (2016, March 6). *Beyond Continuous Monitoring: Threat Modeling for Real-time Response.* Retrieved from SANS Institute: http://www.sans.org/reading-room/whitepapers/analyst/continuous-monitoring-threat-modeling-real-time-response-35185

Sternstein, A. (2015, January 6). *OPM Hackers Skirted Cutting-Edge Intrusion Detection System, Official Says .* Retrieved from Nextgov: http://www.nextgov.com/cybersecurity/2015/06/opm-hackers-skirted-cutting-edge-interior-intrusion-detection-official-says/114649/

APPENDIX D – NIST 800-171 COMPLIANCE CHECKLIST

The following compliance checklist is intended to provide a guide to conduct a "self-assessment" of the company's overall cybersecurity posture as required by NIST 800-171.

*Assessment Method: Refer to NIST 800-171A, *Assessing Security Requirements for Controlled Unclassified Information*, that describes types and means to self-validate the control. The three assessment methods are: examine, interview and test.

Control #	Description	Assessment Method*	Document (e.g., SSP or Co. Procedure Guide)	Page #	Reviewed By	Validated By
Access Control (AC)						
3.1.1	*Limit information system access to authorized users, processes acting on behalf of authorized users, or devices (including other information systems).*					
3.1.2	*Limit information system access to the types of transactions and functions that authorized users are permitted to execute.*					
3.1.3	*Control the flow of CUI in accordance with approved authorizations.*					
3.1.4	*Separate the duties of individuals to reduce the risk of malevolent activity without collusion.*					
3.1.5	*Employ the principle of least privilege, including for specific security functions and privileged accounts.*					
3.1.6	*Use non-privileged accounts or roles when accessing nonsecurity functions.*					
3.1.7	*Prevent non-privileged users from executing privileged functions and audit the execution of such functions.*					
3.1.8	*Limit unsuccessful logon attempts*					
3.1.9	*Provide privacy and security notices consistent with applicable CUI rules.*					
3.1.10	Use *session lock with pattern-hiding displays to prevent access/viewing of data after period of inactivity.*					
3.1.11	*Terminate (automatically) a user session after a defined condition.*					

Control #	Description	Assessment Method*	Document (e.g., SSP or Co. Procedure Guide)	Page #	Reviewed By	Validated By
Access Control (AC)						
3.1.12	*Monitor and control remote access sessions.*					
3.1.13	*Employ cryptographic mechanisms to protect the confidentiality of remote access sessions.*					
3.1.14	*Route remote access via managed access control points.*					
3.1.15	*Authorize remote execution of privileged commands and remote access to security-relevant information.*					
3.1.16	*Authorize wireless access prior to allowing such connections.*					
3.1.17	Protect wireless access using authentication and encryption.					
3.1.18	Control connection of mobile devices.					
3.1.19	Encrypt *CUI on mobile devices.*					
3.1.20	Verify and control/limit connections to and use of external systems.					
3.1.21	Limit use of organizational portable storage devices on external systems.					
3.1.22	Control CUI posted or processed on publicly accessible systems.					

NOTES:_____

_____

_____

Control #	Description	Assessment Method*	Document (e.g., SSP or Co. Procedure Guide)	Page #	Reviewed By	Validated By
Awareness & Training (AT)						
3.2.1	*Ensure that managers, systems administrators, and users of organizational information systems are made aware of the security risks associated with their activities and of the applicable policies, standards, and procedures related to the security of organizational information systems.*					
3.2.2	*Ensure that organizational personnel are adequately trained to carry out their assigned information security-related duties and responsibilities.*					
3.2.3	*Provide security awareness training on recognizing and reporting potential indicators of insider threat.*					

NOTES:_____

_____

_____

_____

_____

_____

Control #	Description	Assessment Method*	Document (e.g., SSP or Co. Procedure Guide)	Page #	Reviewed By	Validated By
Audit & Accountability (AU)						
3.3.1	*Create, protect, and retain information system audit records to the extent needed to enable the monitoring, analysis, investigation, and reporting of unlawful, unauthorized, or inappropriate information system activity.*					
3.3.2	*Ensure that the actions of individual information system users can be uniquely traced to those users so they can be held accountable for their actions*					
3.3.3	*Review and update audited events.*					
3.3.4	*Alert in the event of an audit process failure.*					
3.3.5	*Correlate audit review, analysis, and reporting processes for investigation and response to indications of inappropriate, suspicious, or unusual activity.*					
3.3.6	*Provide audit reduction and report generation to support on-demand analysis and reporting.*					
3.3.7	*Provide an information system capability that compares and synchronizes internal system clocks with an authoritative source to generate time stamps for audit records.*					
3.3.8	*Protect audit information and audit tools from unauthorized access, modification, and deletion.*					
3.3.9	*Limit management of audit functionality to a subset of privileged users.*					

NOTES:_____

_____

_____

_____

_____

_____

Control #	Description	Assessment Method*	Document (e.g., SSP or Co. Procedure Guide)	Page #	Reviewed By	Validated By
Configuration Management (CM)						
3.4.1	Establish and maintain baseline configurations and inventories of organizational information systems (including hardware, software, firmware, and documentation) throughout the respective system development life cycles.					
3.4.2	Establish and enforce security configuration settings for information technology products employed in organizational information systems.					
3.4.3	Track, review, approve/disapprove, and audit changes to information systems.					
3.4.4	Analyze the security impact of changes prior to implementation.					
3.4.5	Define, document, approve, and enforce physical and logical access restrictions associated with changes to the information system.					
3.4.6	Employ the principle of least functionality by configuring the information system to provide only essential capabilities.					
3.4.7	Restrict, disable, and prevent the use of nonessential programs, functions, ports, protocols, and services.					
3.4.8	Apply deny-by-exception (blacklist) policy to prevent the use of unauthorized software or deny all, permit-by-exception (whitelisting) policy to allow the execution of authorized software.					
3.4.9	Control and monitor user-installed software.					

NOTES:_____

_____

_____

_____

_____

Control #	Description	Assessment Method*	Document (e.g., SSP or Co. Procedure Guide)	Page #	Reviewed By	Validated By
Identification & Authentication (IA)						
3.5.1	*Identify information system users, processes acting on behalf of users, or devices.*					
3.5.2	*Authenticate (or verify) the identities of those users, processes, or devices, as a prerequisite to allowing access to organizational information systems.*					
3.5.3	*Use multifactor authentication for local and network access to privileged accounts and for network access to non-privileged accounts.*					
3.5.4	*Employ replay-resistant authentication mechanisms for network access to privileged and nonprivileged accounts.*					
3.5.5	*Prevent reuse of identifiers for a defined period.*					
3.5.6	*Disable identifiers after a defined period of inactivity.*					
3.5.7	*Enforce a minimum password complexity and change of characters when new passwords are created.*					
3.5.8	*Prohibit password reuse for a specified number of generations.*					
3.5.9	*Allow temporary password use for system logons with an immediate change to a permanent password.*					
3.5.10	*Store and transmit only encrypted representation of passwords.*					
3.5.11.	*Obscure feedback of authentication information.*					

NOTES:_____

_____

_____

_____

_____

_____

Control #	Description	Assessment Method*	Document (e.g., SSP or Co. Procedure Guide)	Page #	Reviewed By	Validated By
Incident Response (IR)						
3.6.1	*Establish an operational incident-handling capability for organizational information systems that includes adequate preparation, detection, analysis, containment, recovery, and user response activities.*					
3.6.2	*Track, document, and report incidents to appropriate officials and/or authorities both internal and external to the organization.*					
3.6.3	Test the organizational incident response capability.					

NOTES:_____

_____

_____

_____

_____

Control #	Description	Assessment Method*	Document (e.g., SSP or Co. Procedure Guide)	Page #	Reviewed By	Validated By
Maintenance (MA)						
3.7.1	Perform maintenance on organizational information systems.					
3.7.2	Provide effective controls on the tools, techniques, mechanisms, and personnel used to conduct information system maintenance.					
3.7.3	Ensure equipment removed for off-site maintenance is sanitized of any CUI.					
3.7.4	Check media containing diagnostic and test programs for malicious code before the media are used in the information system.					
3.7.5	Require multifactor authentication to establish nonlocal maintenance sessions via external network connections and terminate such connections when nonlocal maintenance is complete.					
3.7.6	Supervise the maintenance activities of maintenance personnel without required access authorization.					

NOTES:_____

_____

_____

_____

Control #	Description	Assessment Method*	Document (e.g., SSP or Co. Procedure Guide)	Page #	Reviewed By	Validated By
Media Protection (MP)						
3.8.1	*Protect (i.e., physically control and securely store) information system media containing CUI, both paper and digital.*					
3.8.2	*Limit access to CUI on information system media to authorized users.*					
3.8.3	*Sanitize or destroy information system media containing CUI before disposal or release for reuse.*					
3.8.4	*Mark media with necessary CUI markings and distribution limitations.*					
3.8.5	*Control access to media containing CUI and maintain accountability for media during transport outside of controlled areas.*					
3.8.6	*Implement cryptographic mechanisms to protect the confidentiality of CUI stored on digital media during transport unless otherwise protected by alternative physical safeguards.*					
3.8.7	*Control the use of removable media on information system components.*					
3.8.8	*Prohibit the use of portable storage devices when such devices have no identifiable owner.*					
3.8.9	*Protect the confidentiality of backup CUI at storage locations.*					

NOTES:_____

_____

_____

_____

_____

_____

Control #	Description	Assessment Method*	Document (e.g., SSP or Co. Procedure Guide)	Page #	Reviewed By	Validated By
Personnel Security (PS)						
3.9.1	*Screen individuals prior to authorizing access to information systems containing CUI.*					
3.9.2	*Ensure that CUI and information systems containing CUI are protected during and after personnel actions such as terminations and transfers.*					

NOTES:_____

_____

_____

_____

_____

_____

_____

_____

Control #	Description	Assessment Method*	Document (e.g., SSP or Co. Procedure Guide)	Page #	Reviewed By	Validated By
Physical Security (PP)						
3.10.1	*Limit physical access to organizational information systems, equipment, and the respective operating environments to authorized individuals.*					
3.10.2	*Protect and monitor the physical facility and support infrastructure for those information systems.*					
3.10.3	*Escort visitors and monitor visitor activity.*					
3.10.4	*Maintain audit logs of physical access.*					
3.10.5	*Control and manage physical access devices.*					
3.10.6	*Enforce safeguarding measures for CUI at alternate work sites (e.g., telework sites).*					

NOTES:_____

_____

_____

_____

_____

Control #	Description	Assessment Method*	Document (e.g., SSP or Co. Procedure Guide)	Page #	Reviewed By	Validated By
Risk Assessments (RA)						
3.11.1	*Periodically assess the risk to organizational operations (including mission, functions, image, or reputation), organizational assets, and individuals, resulting from the operation of organizational information systems and the associated processing, storage, or transmission of CUI.*					
3.11.2	*Scan for vulnerabilities in the information system and applications periodically and when new vulnerabilities affecting the system are identified.*					
3.11.3	*Remediate vulnerabilities in accordance with assessments of risk.*					

NOTES:_____

_____

_____

_____

_____

Control #	Description	Assessment Method*	Document (e.g., SSP or Co. Procedure Guide)	Page #	Reviewed By	Validated By
Security Assessments (SA)						
3.12.1	Periodically assess the security controls in organizational information systems to determine if the controls are effective in their application.					
3.12.2	*Develop and implement plans of action designed to correct deficiencies and reduce or eliminate vulnerabilities in organizational information systems.*					
3.12.3	Monitor information system security controls on an ongoing basis to ensure the continued effectiveness of the controls.					
3.12.4	Develop, document, and periodically update system security plans that describe system boundaries, system environments of operation, how security requirements are implemented, and the relationships with or connections to other systems.					

NOTES:_____

_____

_____

_____

_____

Control #	Description	Assessment Method*	Document (e.g., SSP or Co. Procedure Guide)	Page #	Reviewed By	Validated By
System & Communications Protection (SC)						
3.13.1	*Monitor, control, and protect organizational communications (i.e., information transmitted or received by organizational information systems) at the external boundaries and key internal boundaries of the information systems.*					
3.13.2	*Employ architectural designs, software development techniques, and systems engineering principles that promote effective information security within organizational information systems.*					
3.13.3	*Separate user functionality from information system management functionality.*					
3.13.4	*Prevent unauthorized and unintended information transfer via shared system resources.*					
3.13.5	*Implement subnetworks for publicly accessible system components that are physically or logically separated from internal networks.*					
3.13.6	*Deny network communications traffic by default and allow network communications traffic by exception (i.e., deny all, permit by exception).*					
3.13.7	*Prevent remote devices from simultaneously establishing non-remote connections with the information system and communicating via some other connection to resources in external networks.*					

Control #	Description	Assessment Method*	Document (e.g., SSP or Co. Procedure Guide)	Page #	Reviewed By	Validated By
System & Communications Protection (SC)						
3.13.8	*Implement cryptographic mechanisms to prevent unauthorized disclosure of CUI during transmission unless otherwise protected by alternative physical safeguards.*					
3.13.9	*Terminate network connections associated with communications sessions at the end of the sessions or after a defined period of inactivity.*					
3.13.10	*Establish and manage cryptographic keys for cryptography employed in the information system.*					
3.13.11	*Employ FIPS-validated cryptography when used to protect the confidentiality of CUI.*					
3.13.12	*Prohibit remote activation of collaborative computing devices and provide indication of devices in use to users present at the device.*					
3.13.13	*Control and monitor the use of mobile code.*					
3.13.14	*Control and monitor the use of Voice over Internet Protocol (VoIP) technologies.*					
3.13.15	*Protect the authenticity of communications sessions.*					
3.13.16	*Protect the confidentiality of CUI at rest.*					

NOTES:_____

_____

Control #	Description	Assessment Method*	Document	Page #	Reviewed By	Validated By
System & Information Integrity (SI)						
3.14.1	*Identify, report, and correct information and information system flaws in a timely manner.*					
3.14.2	*Provide protection from malicious code at appropriate locations within organizational information systems.*					
3.14.3	*Monitor information system security alerts and advisories and take appropriate actions in response.*					
3.14.4	*Update malicious code protection mechanisms when new releases are available.*					
3.14.5	*Perform periodic scans of the information system and real-time scans of files from external sources as files are downloaded, opened, or executed.*					
3.14.6	*Monitor the information system including inbound and outbound communications traffic, to detect attacks and indicators of potential attacks.*					
3.14.7	*Identify unauthorized use of the information system*					

NOTES:_____

_____

_____

_____

ABOUT THE AUTHOR

Mr. Russo is currently the Senior Information Security Engineer within the Department of Defense's (DOD) F-35 Joint Strike Fighter program. He has an extensive background in cybersecurity and is an expert in the Risk Management Framework (RMF) and DOD Instruction 8510 which implements RMF throughout the DOD and federal government. He holds both a Certified Information Systems Security Professional (CISSP) certification and a CISSP in information security architecture (ISSAP). He holds a 2017 certification as a Chief Information Security Officer (CISO) from the National Defense University, Washington, DC. He retired from the US Army Reserves in 2012 as the Senior Intelligence Officer.

He is the former CISO at the Department of Education where in 2016 he led the effort to close over 95% of the outstanding US Congressional and Inspector General cybersecurity shortfall weaknesses spanning as far back as five years.

Mr. Russo is the former Senior Cybersecurity Engineer supporting the Joint Medical Logistics Development Functional Center of the Defense Health Agency (DHA) at Fort Detrick, MD. He led a team of engineering and cybersecurity professionals protecting five major Medical Logistics systems supporting over 200 DOD Medical Treatment Facilities around the globe.

In 2011, Mr. Russo was certified by the Office of Personnel Management as a graduate of the Senior Executive Service Candidate program.

From 2009 through 2011, Mr. Russo was the Chief Technology Officer at the Small Business Administration (SBA). He led a team of over 100 IT professionals in supporting an intercontinental Enterprise IT infrastructure and security operations spanning 12-time zones; he deployed cutting-edge technologies to enhance SBA's business and information sharing operations supporting the small business community. Mr. Russo was the first-ever Program Executive Officer (PEO)/Senior Program Manager in the Office of Intelligence & Analysis at Headquarters, Department of Homeland Security (DHS), Washington, DC. Mr. Russo was responsible for the development and deployment of secure Information and Intelligence support systems for OI&A to include software applications and systems to enhance the DHS mission. He was responsible for the program management development lifecycle during his tenure at DHS.

He holds a Master of Science from the National Defense University in Government Information Leadership with a concentration in Cybersecurity and a Bachelor of Arts in Political Science with a minor in Russian Studies from Lehigh University. He holds Level III Defense Acquisition certification in Program Management, Information Technology, and Systems Engineering. He has been a member of the DOD Acquisition Corps since 2001.

One Year After OPM Data Breach, What Has the Government Learned?

*"...The agency now requires employees to use **two-factor authentication** to log into their computers, meaning a password and a secure card. Employees can no longer access their Gmail ® accounts from their office computers. OPM has also implemented new tools to detect malware. ...[T]he government can see all the devices connected to its networks as well as monitor the data moving into and out of the system."*
(SOURCE: https://www.npr.org/sections/alltechconsidered/2016/06/06/480968999/one-year-after-opm-data-breach-what-has-the-government-learned)

www.ingramcontent.com/pod-product-compliance
Lightning Source LLC
LaVergne TN
LVHW012316070326
832902LV00004BA/75